VERA AND ELLY'S WAR

SAM SMITH

BeWrite Books, UK
www.bewrite.net

Published internationally by BeWrite Books, UK.
363 Badminton Road, Nibley, Bristol. BS37 5JF.

British Library Cataloguing in Publication Data.
A catalogue record for this book is available from the British Library

ISBN 1-904224-97-0

Digitally produced by BeWrite Books.

Cover design by Caitlin Myers

For

Stephanie

Stephen

Christopher

Author photograph by Sarah Hibbert.

Prolific author, Sam Smith, has a number of novels and poetry collections to his credit. One novel 'Sister Blister' was entered for the 2000 Booker Prize; another, 'The End of Science Fiction', was short-listed for a 2001 Eppie.

His innovative detective novels, 'Marks' and 'Porlock Counterpoint' are now available at BeWrite Books as is his groundbreaking work 'Care Vortex'.

A WW2 babe, Sam presently lives in Ilfracombe, in the English South West, where the local paper described him as a 'creative genius'.

Sam Smith is also publisher and editor of the poetry and review magazine, The Journal, and the poetry press 'Original Plus'; as well as British liaisons link to River King Poetry Supplement (USA). Contact him at: SmithsssJ@aol.com.

Vera and Eddy's War is based on in-depth interviews with the couple and is accurate according to Vera and Eddy's memories of the events and characters described.

VERA AND EDDY'S WAR

Introduction

My father was serving in the Royal Air Force, my mother was a WAAF (Women's Auxiliary Air Force). That is how they met. I was born in 1946. 'The War' was the background, the whole history, to my becoming.

I grew up in Devon, England, at Stoke Gabriel on the River Dart estuary. My earliest awareness of 'The War', apart from the sideboard photographs of my mother and father in uniform, was due to a travelling cinema that visited the village hall (then in Church Walk). Flickering newsreel footage of war devastation, of the concentration camps, was followed by war films starring Kenneth More, Audie Murphy and the like.

Short trips out of the village to Paignton and Torquay showed war damage – timber-shored gaps in terraces, jigsaws of wallpaper, fireplaces still suspended. Longer trips to Plymouth to visit elderly relatives revealed nearly a whole city being rebuilt.

Paul Meadow, down-river from Stoke Gabriel, had been the site of an American wartime camp. As boys we foraged there for cannon and cartridge shells. The unspent we put in a vice and tried to detonate with a nail and hammer, fortunately without success. Once emptied, we polished up the brass casings and used them as ornaments.

My father, in an attempt, I think, to bring home to us the immensity of it all, bought for my brother and I a history of the war in pictures that ran to several volumes.

He wanted, he said, to show us what he had been fighting against – that is, the damage done by the Germans to cities like Plymouth; and to Coventry, London, Liverpool, Southampton,

Exeter, Bristol, etcetera. He showed me too, with pride, the rubble his Lancaster bombers (he was a Lancastrian) had created of places like Cologne and Berlin.

I saw also in those volumes, and became obsessed by, factors that he hadn't known at the time, and which hadn't been part of the justification for his 'going to war' – the photographs of Belsen's pits, of the ovens at Auschwitz, of the casual hangings. That human beings could so treat one another ... And all the while, in my growing up (TV had come along) I was continually shown the blackened street plan of Hiroshima, a mushroom cloud rising.

Add to that mix the normal growing up family resentments – I, self-centred as any teenager, resenting every expectation placed upon me, especially those I felt to be inappropriate to my time, to my peace-time; while my parents seemed to resent my not having known their war, not having known their struggles ... In me, subsequently, grew a real need – as defensive armour possibly, but a definite need nonetheless – to understand the war that had created me. My questions, however, and simply because I was questioning, made me seem irreverent.

Both my parents were proud of having belonged to their branch of the Armed forces. On Remembrance Days, both pinned on their medals and marched with the British Legion, my mother being promoted one time to standard bearer. But that was only one day a year. For the rest of the year they seemed to be estranged within the small village, and uncomfortable with their fluctuating status within civilian life. Both, consequently, owned a nostalgia for the communal privations and *camaraderie* of wartime.

My father's bravery was beyond question. Invalided out of the RAF, he had immediately signed up for the Royal Navy, had seen out the war serving on a destroyer shepherding Murmansk convoys. His stories about 'The War', however, offered little enlightenment to its cause, and conveyed little of how it had felt being caught up in it.

When he did choose to talk about it, his stories always had a forceful point – political or moral. Often I felt that I, in my apparent irreverence and ingratitude, was being held to blame for all those 'who hadn't made it back'. Even when the intention didn't seem to be to make me feel guilty, both my mother and father's war stories were straight out of a wartime propaganda machine, were newspaper nationalistic and jingoistic, slogan become myth. And their friends, being their friends, were also the kind of people who instantly took sides; and so their stories were the same. While my easygoing uncles, not wanting to usurp my father's authoritative version, could not be drawn on their time as commandos or working on bomb disposal ...

Trying to find out what it might have been like for someone like me to have been in that war, I became, of course, susceptible to alternative views. I met men who had felt compassion for the fellow sailors they had just blasted out of the water; similarly Spitfire pilots who, imagining the effect, had winced at the cannon-shell they fired into Messerschmitts and Stukas. I met men who, post-war, had become infatuated with Japanese culture after their time spent as Japanese POWs. I met men who, as conscientious objectors, had insisted on being sent to jail rather than contribute to the 'war effort'. A village 'aunty' told of now-respectable village women sneaking through the woods to the American camp in Paul Meadow; and returning with rolls of lavatory paper, tins of peaches, chocolate bars. One woman was even seen struggling back with a whole side of beef. I worked with men who had served in wars since 'The War', and who had shaken their heads at the carnage, at their being 'politically' used.

But each tale, somehow, although all equally valid, had been but a singular point of view, often self-glorifying, and were either too personal or, like my parents', not personal enough.

Of course I also read histories of 'The War', political analyses of events leading up to it, consequences of it. Analyses that again were more or less valid viewpoints, but which didn't offer a human picture of 'The War'. H.H. Kirst, C.S. Forrester, John Steinbeck, Gunter Grass, Kurt Vonnegut, all offered insights. And then I read Eric Linklater, who said that the most any one book of 'The War' could be was 'but a dotted line across a map of the war.'

So I gave up trying to justify my own life with regard to 'The War', and I got on with living.

Vera and Eddy became my in-laws. Eddy talked – a lot. And he talked of his war – a lot. It was a family joke before I was a part of the family. Other conversations continued around him, while he talked. When Eddy's and the general topic coincided, Vera might amend his stories. Eddy might then defend his version, or it might send him off on another tack ... Occasionally, when everyone else had left the room, Eddy would still be sitting there, talking.

About his war.

One day I listened …

One

Pre-War: Histories & Meetings

Vera Lucy Avery was born on June 6th 1914. Lucy was her mother's maiden name, and she was called Vera after an aunt.

Whereas her mother, father and sister, Doll, were all dark, Vera had white blonde hair. As a toddler she was so tiny that her father, Ned, was able to stand her in a biscuit barrel on the bar.

Her mother and father had acquired the Globe Hotel because Ned had been head groom to the Strubins up on the moors. Strubins was a self-made man, had made his money digging diamonds in South Africa. The Strubins had wanted Ned to go with them to the mines in South Africa. Vera's mother, though, having been pregnant with Doll, hadn't wanted to go. So, as they had with all their other staff who had not wanted to go with them, the Strubins set Ned up in his own business.

Vera's mother was a beautiful woman of Italian descent. She had thick black wavy hair and deepset hazel eyes, was tall and slender. Before her marriage to Ned she had been a lady's maid, having started as an under nanny in service. And she was artistic. Mrs Strubins had once asked her to make floral arrangements for the dining room as Dame Clara Butt, the opera singer, and many other theatricals were coming for the weekend.

"I want you to do something unusual," Mrs Strubins had told her.

"Let me do just what I want," Vera's mother had said.

"Tell the gardeners, Helen, that I said you're to have whatever you like."

Vera's mother, though, did not go near the gardens; she went to the fields and picked ripe corn, wild poppies and cornflowers. From those she made the table pieces. All the weekend's visiting artistes praised her originality.

Before the Strubins, Vera's mother had been maid to Lady Coventry. Lady Coventry had been a flirt. Vera's mother had kept watch on her assignations – out of affection and concern. One day she heard Lady Coventry cry out and dashed to her rescue. One of the men had tried to kiss her.

Vera's mother was an innocent.

Most of their first customers at the Globe Hotel were Australian troops – billeted on them during the Great War.

Although Ned had tried to enlist in the Royal Navy he had failed the medical – they had said that he had too much fat around his heart. Yet when he was drunk Ned could do a Cossack dance.

He was a big strong man who liked a fight. Forty-six inches around the chest unexpanded, he saw himself as a real John Bull. During the Great War he had tried to enlist again and again, and each time he had been rejected.

When Vera was five her mother and father sold up the Globe Hotel and moved to the Palk Arms in Ellacombe. The Palk Arms had the reputation of being a very rough house. The first week there, the customers put Ned to the test. He threw three headfirst down the six steep front steps. He had no trouble after that.

Vera and her sister, Doll, were both sent to Dalminio's, a private school in Abbey Road. Doll fared better than Vera. Vera had to wear glasses. Her retinas were almond-shaped instead of circular, so that, without glasses, she saw too much – stars looked like moons. Even so, Vera was a compulsive reader – and she did not help her eyes reading by candlelight: they had no electricity in the top two floors of Palk Arms.

On leaving school, Vera became a hairdresser, began her apprenticeship in Sidney Smith's – a salon in Union Street, just around the corner from the bottom of Market Street. Her mother and father had to pay a premium of £25 for her to become an apprentice. Her own hair was a frizzy blonde with reddish lights.

Mr Smith was a thin man, unfailingly polite and kind. He had been wigmaker to old bald Queen Mary. He taught Vera and Rene wigmaking.

Rene's parents had been regulars at the Palk Arms, had brought Rene to sleep there most nights with Vera. They had grown up together. Mr Smith called Rene 'Miss Sarah'. That gave Vera and Rene the giggles. It did not take much to give Vera and Rene the giggles.

Edwin John Dart was born in Kingskerswell on February 6th 1910. He was named after his father and his grandfather. Kingskerswell was a small village midway between Torquay and Newton Abbot.

Eddy caught pneumonia as a baby, had it twice more before he was six years old. His mother was unable to look after him, so he was sent to live with a doctor and his family.

When Eddy was four years old, his father had gone away to the Great War in the Far East. After staying with the doctor's family, Eddy was sent to Chudleigh – at the head of the Teign Valley – to live with his Grandmother Gill. His mother worked as a taxi driver and barmaid to pay for his keep. He was the only child.

Also at Granny Gill's were two of his cousins from London. Their mother, Aunt Lydia, was a peculiar yellow colour. The school she had been teaching in had been blown up in a zeppelin raid and the plaster dust had stained her skin.

The school at Chudleigh was full of farm boys. Eddy had to fight or go under. Whenever his mother found out that he had been fighting, she gave him a hammering. Her own brothers were still frightened of her. She sent Eddy to ballet classes.

Eddy's grandfather, Gill, was a carter. Eddy went with him, hauling lumber from Haldon moor, or taking the turnstile from Chudleigh to Taunton races and bringing it back again.

Eddy's father came back from the war in the East, was immediately sent to Ireland with the Black and Tans to subdue the rebellious Irish. When at last he arrived home, Eddy went down to meet him at Chudleigh station. His mother also took along two other boys Eddy's age – Mill Millman and Tucket. Had Eddy's mother not pointed Eddy out, his father would not have known which of the three boys was his.

Eddy was ten years old when he went to live with his mother and father in Newton Abbot, at 34, Buller Road. He was sent first to a school run by nuns, then – when he was eleven – to Bell's, the Church of England school. His father, like his father before him who had been a master potter, returned to work in the pottery. Eddy's father was a handler – he put handles and spouts on the teapots – while his brother Fred made the shapes.

Eddy's father suffered recurring bouts of malaria and shellshock, came out in sweats. Eddy gave up ballet lessons, took to throwing lumps of turf at the local policeman, chucking pepper in church, and was taught to box as his father had been taught before him.

When Eddy was fourteen his mother gave birth to a boy, Jim. When Eddy was fifteen she gave birth to a girl. Eddy began playing in a band.

Eddy had always enjoyed knocking a couple of sticks about a tin, had progressed to a skittle drum. A few older lads had started a dance band in Newton Abbot. Frank Andrews played the piano, Dick – an older man who worked on the railway – played the fiddle; and Dick Sanders – an ex–soldier from the Great War – played a one-string fiddle with a horn on it. Timo Gilpin was the West of England cornet champion and came from a musical family.

The band's only one-step was 'Pasadena'. All the others were quicksteps – 'I'm one of the nuts of Barcelona' and 'Valencia'. They were also competent enough in the 'Lancers' and the 'Valleta'.

New Year's Eve found the band playing in Bickington village hall. Eddy was at the dance. The drummer was taken ill. The set of drums were there – a one-sided big drum, a one–sided side drum and an assortment of percussion; as well as a box of odd instruments, such as a swanee whistle for waltzes, a whistle full of water for birdsong; and a clog box, triangle, etcetera. They asked Eddy to stand in.

That night Eddy proved himself just about competent; and, although he was still only fifteen, the band took him on. His mother was a bit doubtful, but he was allowed to go, and was paid eight bob (shillings) for playing from eight until two in the morning. Hunt balls went on until three.

Eddy was fascinated by the fiddle player, who he knew had a wife and children. But the fiddle player wasn't on the stage half the time. He would play a couple of tunes, then disappear outside with a woman. And Timo Gilpin always had a small barrel of beer beside him. Neither he nor Dick Sanders would play without one; it was included in the price.

Eddy got himself another evening job; at the cinema, creating sound effects behind the screen. A German orchestra played there. It was all one family except for the drummer who was called Reece, an ex-RAF man. Reece had a complete set of tympani; and it was he who taught Eddy all the tricks of the trade.

The band dropped the cornet player – he got too fond of the beer – and they went from strength to strength, were out playing almost every night. Friday nights they played Chudleigh, the next night Staverton, the next Stoke Gabriel, then Landscove, Denbury, Ipplepen. The band had a following that travelled in coaches. And in every village hall two tables were set aside for the old farmers who played nap card games for money throughout the evening.

Eddy's baby sister had been born with a hole in her heart. She only lived until she was eleven months old. His mother died. She was forty two. Six months afterwards, his brother died. The doctor said that he had simply pined away.

Eddy and his father moved into lodgings in St Marychurch Road, Milbur, just outside Newton Abbot. Following his mother's wishes Eddy had entered an architect's office. Evenings he played the drums in the dance band; weekends he went fishing.

When Eddy was seventeen, he was playing in the band in Ford Hall, Newton Abbot. A boxer from London kept thumping Eddy's bass drum every time he passed it. Eddy threatened him. He was threatened back. They agreed to settle it in the ring. The fight was to be part of a charity programme in the Palace Hotel, Torquay. During the days before the fight Eddy was backed by several people. And, unknown to Eddy, his father watched the fight. Eddy won, made himself a bit of money.

Eddy disliked working indoors. Realising that, because he didn't have the connections, he would always be an office boy, Eddy left the architect's office to become a mason.

In 1933 Vera was nineteen years old. She had many boyfriends. Norman Weed thought that he was Vera's only boyfriend. She was with him in the Empire Cinema when she first saw Eddy.

Eddy and Sissie were sitting in the row in front of her and Norman. Norman watched the film – 'The Singing Fool' – while Vera studied Eddy and Sissie. They were supposed to be the best looking couple in Newton Abbot.

Eddy was tall, had a straight nose, a thin black moustache and pale blue eyes. Sissie had auburn hair. Throughout the film Eddy and Sissie quarrelled: Vera thought that they might both be very good-looking, but they weren't half bad-tempered.

Ron Pouilly was now playing in the band with Eddy. One night Eddy discovered that Ron was going to take Sissie out after they had finished playing. So, during the break, Eddy sneaked out of the dance hall and down a back street to where Ron had parked his car – an MG sports. Smashing a milk bottle, Eddy jammed it under his front tyre.

What a rotten sod I am, Eddy thought to himself. *I should've stayed and knocked his block off.*

A few days later, Ron told Eddy that his tyre had been punctured in three places.

"What rotten sod would play a dirty trick like that?" Eddy said.

The back of Sidney Smith's looked down on Pimlico. One of Vera's customers was a mousy little girl. Her boyfriend drove a grocer's van. While she had her hair done, the boyfriend would wait out back in the van. One day Rene grabbed hold of Vera.

"Quick! Quick!" She dragged Vera upstairs to the back window. From there they could see down into the van's cab. The boyfriend was masturbating.

After that they, giggling, watched out for him. And every day, while waiting for his girlfriend, he masturbated.

They made their shampoo in that upstairs back room – boiling up buckets of pure soap and adding scent. At first those doing it had kept an eye out for the boyfriend, had called the other girls over when he had arrived. In the end they got sick of it. One day they opened the window and emptied a bucket of hot shampoo over him. That was the last they saw of him.

Sissie's parents owned a fish and chip shop in Newton Abbot. Sissie's mother was the guiding force, bossed Sissie's father about. One Sunday afternoon Sissie started to nag Eddy like her mother nagged her father.

Eddy knocked Sissie over the living room sofa and walked out.

Mr Smith sold out and moved to Bournemouth. A Mr Dingle took over the shop. Up until then most of Vera's customers had come from the Palk Arms. If she worked late Mr Smith would give her a day off in lieu. Mr Smith had been polite to her pub customers. They, however, were not the kind of customers Mr Dingle wanted.

Mr Dingle was a fat man with a little moustache. On taking over the shop he immediately put the prices up. What with that and his being rude to them, soon Vera's customers would not come into the shop. They asked Vera to do their hair for them at home. So, not wanting to lose her customers, she did their hair after work in the Palk Arms bathroom.

The Co-op Hall dance was a roughhouse. Even so, Eddy was banned twice from it. In the 'ladies excuse me', a big brute of a redheaded Scotsman was in the habit of slamming the man in possession aside. He did it to Frank Andrews a couple of times. Eddy saw him coming up behind him. He ducked and swung around.

"I wouldn't try that again," Eddy warned.

"I'll see you outside," the Scotsman growled down at him.

"Right," Eddy said.

Ethel Stormon held onto him. "You can't go out there. He'll kill you."

Eddy had a black trilby he wore cocked over one eye. PC Banks, the local policeman, was on the door.

"I think you're taking on a bit there boy," he said to Eddy. "He's a big rough bugger." PC Banks had taught Eddy to box. "You goin' to have a go?" Eddy nodded.

"Well if he gets too bad," PC Banks said, "I'll arrest him. But if you're beatin' him I won't say anythin' about it."

Eddy was first outside. As the Scotsman came out, Eddy brushed off his trilby with one hand and banged him with the other. The Scotsman hadn't expected it, and Eddy didn't give him a chance to recover, got stuck in and down he went. As Eddy triumphantly walked away something exploded in the back of his head.

He came to in Torbay hospital, could not understand why he was farting so much. He couldn't seem to stop; and on the back of his head was a lump the size of an egg. And still he couldn't stop farting. The doctor told him that it was because he had concussion. He would have to stay in hospital the night.

"What did he hit you with?"

"No idea," Eddy said, listening to himself farting.

Frank picked him up in the morning. Eddy asked him what had happened. The Scotsman's girlfriend had hit him with her umbrella. It had had a carved cock's head on the handle.

Vera and Eddy both went to a party at Gwen Twose's house. Vera went with Norman Weed.

The fashion for girls then was a beret over one eye and costumes – a suit with a long fitted jacket – worn with a cravat. Vera had one suit in strawberry pink, which she wore with a monogrammed cravat. Another suit she had was a mustard colour, which she wore with brown accessories. The shoes were open-toed with straps across the instep. And the hair was swept back and pulled forward into a quiff.

Eddy went to the party with Gwen Shorts. Gwen Twose's father was a policeman and a teetotaller. He didn't allow drink in the house. The men had bottles of whisky hidden in the lavatory cistern. PC Twose said that he had never seen such a happy party.

Vera's father hated Twose: PC Twose was too conscientious by far. Men would come rushing into the Palk Arms: "Quick Ned! PC Twose is on his way." So Ned would have to close early, at the legal closing time.

A dedicated policeman, PC Twose would have arrested his own wife. She knew about the whisky in the lavatory cistern.

Postman's Knock was played at the party. After a while Vera and Eddy so managed it that they kept going outside together. Vera thought Eddy a very good kisser. Eddy thought that Norman Weed had no idea what was going on.

Eddy did not have a car, and when the party finished Norman offered Eddy and Gwen Shorts a lift home. Vera was staying the night with Gwen Twose.

Norman first drove Eddy up to Milbur, where he was still in lodgings with his father; and, having dropped Eddy off, Norman then drove Gwen Shorts home – all the way to the other end of town.

Thinking that Norman had only taken Vera to the party, Eddy had arranged to meet her on the Wednesday. But when he found out that Vera was Norman's girl, he sent a message to her, via Gwen Twose, saying that he wouldn't go out with another man's girl; but, if she finished with Norman Weed, then he would. *Who the hell does he think he's ordering about?* Vera thought.

Vera finished with Norman Weed anyway. Norman didn't want to be finished with and followed Vera to a dance at the town hall. Eddy was there. He was drunk. It was his birthday and he hadn't had a birthday card from anyone. He hadn't even seen his father, not since the day, weeks before, when he had come home and found his father holding their landlady upside-down by her ankles and banging her head on the kitchen's stone floor.

At the town hall, Eddy had been supposed to be dancing in a competition with Ethel Stormon. He danced every dance except the competition dance with Vera. Long John told Eddy that he shouldn't be dancing with Vera, that Norman Weed was watching them. Eddy went for a drink and Jack Ness told him that he shouldn't dance with Vera. Eddy knocked Jack down. Jack knocked Eddy down. Come the competition dance Eddy was so drunk that Ethel had to hold him up.

"For Chrissakes stand up. You're drunk as a fart." And Ethel told Eddy that she'd been knitting him a lovely pullover, but now he couldn't have it; she would give it to her father instead.

Vera felt sorry for Eddy. She thought, *Poor bugger. He's falling all over me, so I'd better let him take me home.*

For his first date with her, Eddy was to call for Vera at Dingle's. He had promised not to be drunk. But that Saturday afternoon he went out with Frank Andrews in his Austin Seven. A tiny bricklayer called Sam Avery went along with them. Sam had asthma.

Starting with a drink at the Union, Saturday lunchtime, they then took a few more drinks with them to a Torquay United soccer game. From there, they went to Sam's house, down in Upton, for a cream tea. Sam's father said that they were some relation to Vera's parents. At opening time, Frank, Eddy and Sam went for a few more drinks. Eddy told them that he had to meet Vera to take her to the dance up at the Co-op Hall.

Vera was waiting at the back of the shop for him. The Salvation Army band was playing there – it was their regular pitch.

Eddy had on a pair of plus-four trousers like golfers wore in those days. Just as they pulled up the car, Sam said he felt sick.

"Don't be sick in the bloody car," Eddy said and bundled him out the door. Sam fell smack in the middle of the Salvation Army band and puked.

Vera looked none too pleased.

Eddy and Frank picked Sam up, wiped off the worst, and stuffed him back in the car. Vera got in, and they drove up to the Co-op Hall. Inside the hall, it was very hot. As he danced with Vera, Eddy felt himself becoming ill. Sam had recovered by this time, had cleaned himself up, though he still stank like a pig.

"I've got to go outside," Eddy told Vera. "I feel bad."

Outside the hall was an archway. The dustbins were kept under there. Eddy knew that if he wasn't quick he would shit his pants. Pulling down his plus-fours, he balanced over an empty dustbin. But no sooner had he sat over the dustbin than he was sick, as well as shitting himself. And the more he was sick, the weaker he became, and the further he slid down the dustbin.

PC Banks came out for a breath of air.

"My Christ! What a stink!" He peered under the dark archway. "Who's that?"

"It's me," Eddy said.

"Who's me?"

"Eddy."

"Bloody hell! Jesus! What the hell you doin' of?"

"I'm drunk," Eddy said. "And I can't get out of this dustbin. But I haven't got down to where it is yet."

PC Banks pulled him out; and, feeling better, Eddy had a wash. Then he went back in to find Vera. But she would have nothing more to do with him.

"First and last," she said.

First and last of many.

The following week, Eddy was playing in the band in the Newton Abbot Liberal Club. Norman Poke was the pianist. He was a solicitor's clerk and a bit of a Mary-Anne. Norman Weed came in a side door with his henchman, Long John, a tall Cockney plasterer. With his back to the dancers, and facing the band, Norman Weed unbuttoned his jacket to reveal an army Colt.

"If you don't stay away from Vera," he told Eddy, "I'll bloody use it." Norman Poke had stopped playing.

The band missed six beats.

Norman Weed left by the side door.

"Somebody else play the bloody drums," Eddy said. "I'll kill the bastard. Coming in here threatening me with his bloody gun."

"I wouldn't push him," one of the band warned. "The silly bugger's daft enough to pull the trigger."

What with working at Dingle's during the day and at home on her own customers in the evenings, Vera was dog-tired. A jeweller's shop came up for rent in Alexander Road, just along from the Palk Arms. Borrowing the money for the driers from her mother, Vera set herself up in business. And to get herself established she worked from nine in the morning to nine at night. The shop was rented from Lewish, the fish people. Vera called it 'Maison Vee's'.

In Torquay, Eddy was told that Norman Weed was after him. All Vera's other boyfriends had been frightened off or beaten up by Norman. He was known as The Terror of Ellacombe, was thickset and heavier than Eddy, and he too used to box. Eddy, though, wasn't much bothered, looked upon Norman as only a rough-and-tumble fighter. So it was with Eddy that Vera went to the Ambulance Ball at the Town Hall.

At half-time Vera and Eddy went for a drink in the packed bar downstairs. Norman Weed and the Cockney plasterer were there. Long John had on a red shirt. He saw Vera and Eddy and came over for a chat. Norman came up to Long John.

"You don't want to talk to a thing like her."

Norman had downed a few drinks. He was wearing a dinner jacket and a stiff-collared shirt. Eddy had on a new black suit with a polka-dot tie, and a shirt he had bought in London.

Having realised what Norman had said, Eddy went marching over to him. Norman had his back to Eddy. Long John was facing him. As Eddy reached them, Long John gave Norman the nod. Norman turned and hit Eddy. Eddy went crashing over five tables. His eye thumped so much that he thought, at first, it had been knocked out.

Norman usually only had to hit anyone once for the fight to be over. But Eddy got up off the floor, started to pick up a table to brain Norman with. Vera was quaking.

The dance was being run by the landlord of the Torbay Inn. He grabbed hold of Eddy, told him to get Norman outside. Eddy had once boxed at the Torbay Inn. He told the landlord he could only see out of one eye.

"Never mind that," the landlord told him. "You can still beat him."

"I'm not finished yet," Eddy called out to Norman. "Outside."

Vera stayed inside with Rene. The rest of the dance followed Norman and Eddy onto a patch of grass beside the Town Hall. PC Banks kept order, watched to see fair play. Eddy started to remove his shirt. Norman tore the sleeves off it. Eddy wasn't pleased, swore at Norman. Norman piled in. Eddy ducked off to one side and hit him under the heart. He had learned to do that with a stronger opponent. And whenever Norman charged at Eddy, Eddy dodged aside and jabbed Norman under the heart.

Unable to hit Eddy, Norman roared with frustration, tore his own dinner jacket apart and chucked the two halves away. When the stiff-collared shirt followed, Eddy could see the dark bruise under Norman's heart. He hit him there again. And again. Come the end, Eddy had to pick Norman up to knock him down. Norman tried to crawl up Eddy's legs. Eddy punched him down.

Eddy was bruised, his shirt armless. Back in the Town Hall, he had a drink. Vera wanted to be taken home. Eddy would not go. An hour later PC Banks sent someone to fetch Eddy: Norman hadn't come around. He was still lying out there on the grass, cold as marble with a large black patch growing around his heart. Norman's brothers arrived. Eddy's friends went out to see them in case they cut up rough. Norman's brothers took him to the hospital. Not until late that night did he regain consciousness.

At last, Vera was free of Norman Weed. But now Eddy wanted to be serious, and Eddy had only to look at a man for that man to stop talking to Vera. Eddy had replaced Norman as the kingpin of Ellacombe. So now Vera had to dodge Eddy.

That summer, Eddy was playing every evening in a band at St Marychurch town hall for a man called All White, who came from Ireland. He was a champion dancer, wore white tails, had fair, curly hair and looked a bit of a dude till you came to weigh him up. Then you saw he was six foot two.

On finishing work, Vera used to go alone to the dance. While Eddy played, Vera had a lovely time. Eddy Coraline and many others danced with her. She was never short of partners. Then all of a sudden Eddy Coraline stopped dancing with her; and no-one else asked her to dance.

Eddy had been watching her – all cool and proper while she had danced past the band, then as soon as she'd reached the far end of the hall, where she thought Eddy couldn't see her, she had been all over her partner.

Vera found out that Eddy had warned all the men off. She told him that she wasn't having any of that and walked down to the Spa ballroom. Eddy didn't see her for about four weeks.

Vera went on her own to a Town Hall dance. Ron Pouilly was playing in the band. All the girls were mad about him. He asked Vera if he could take her home.

Vera had on a new dress. It was apple-green pan velvet, off the shoulders, with an edging of fur around the bodice. After the dance, she waited outside the Town Hall for Ron. It was raining. Gladys Stormon came along. She asked Vera who she was waiting for.

"Ron Pouilly."

"Oh you won't get home with him," Gladys said. "He's got a caravan out Maidencombe. All the girls go out there."

"Oh," Vera said, "I'm off." Gladys decided to go with her. The rain was bucketing down.

Just then, Robin called to them from his car. He was a commercial traveller. Gladys fancied him. Vera knew him from her shop. As they were crossing the road to him, George Berry came along. He was a friend of Eddy's. George was very wealthy. His family owned the mills at Buckfastleigh.

George and Robin agreed to see both girls home. Vera was staying at Molly Dawes', one of the girls who worked for her. It was a ruse to avoid Norman Weed, who was still haunting the Palk Arms.

Robin's car only had two doors. Gladys got in the back with George. Vera sat beside Robin.

"Straight up Milbur Downs," George told Robin.

"I'm not going up Milbur Downs," Gladys said.

Robin turned to her. "Boy, oh boy," he said. "Are you two going to be bugged tonight."

That was the first time Vera had heard the word 'bugged'. Neither of the girls had realised Robin was so drunk. In the back, Gladys got hysterical, demanded to be let out of the car, screamed and kicked.

As they came to the harbour Vera glimpsed a man standing by the cockle stall.

"There's my father! Dad! Dad!" she yelled out the window. Robin stopped the car, opened Vera's door, put his foot in her back and sent her sprawling into the mud. Gladys was thrown after her, and the car drove off.

The rain was still pelting down. Picking themselves up, Vera and Gladys dragged themselves over to the shelter of William & Cox's doorway. Gladys fainted.

"Oh don't faint," Vera said. "I don't know what to do." Gladys eventually recovered and they started walking home.

Gladys lived at Torre and so could walk home along the main street. But Molly Dawes lived up the Braddons. The arrangement was that Vera would meet Molly at the top of the creepy steps and then they would go in together so that Molly's mother would think they had chaperoned one another. Molly was man mad. Freezing cold, leaking wet, Vera waited, and waited. Molly arrived at about two o'clock. Vera then had to tell her all that had happened.

Many girls said to Vera: "You going out with Eddy Dart? He's got an awful reputation. He'll do you, alright."

Vera was afraid of him. But if she and Eddy went out on their own he took her to the pictures. When he did eventually take her to some woods, she was half afraid of what he might do. But he didn't try to do anything at all. Vera was most disappointed.

Eddy's reputation, though, was based more on his drinking than his chasing women. In his opinion those women who did, weren't worth having, and why bother with those who wouldn't?

Frank Andrews used to have the women. Women liked him. Baby Face he was called. Often, after a night out, Eddy would be sozzled at three in the morning in Frank's car waiting until Frank had finished with a woman.

Frank went out with a girl who lived up the Teign valley. She was called Crystal. She already had another boyfriend. Eddy was with them when Frank took her home. Her other boyfriend had told Crystal's father what a bad reputation Frank had. Immediately Crystal got out of the car, her father set about her with a Harry Lauder walking stick. Having beaten her to the ground, he next whacked Frank on either side of his head. Then he came for Eddy. But Eddy ducked under the walking stick, grabbed him by the balls, and down he went.

When the village policeman saw what Crystal's father had done to her, he was all for having a go at him himself. (Afterwards, because he'd been such a pig to Crystal and no-one would have anything to do with him, Crystal's father drowned himself in a flooded quarry.)

Frank's next girlfriend was a private nurse to an old gentleman. She was a smart piece, and a sex maniac. Frank couldn't give her enough. She said to Frank: "What about Eddy? Can't he come as well?"

Vera and Eddy made up a foursome with Frank and his girl. They went out to Maidencombe, parted in the woods. In the woods, Vera could hear Frank and the nurse doing it. She was most embarrassed, didn't know where to look in front of Eddy. She wouldn't let Eddy do anything like that. Although, this time, Eddy did try.

Vera told Eddy lies. At Easter, to put him off, she told him that she was going to visit her grandmother. Her grandmother was dead. That afternoon she met a boy from Sealhayne College. He had a sports car. They drove through Newton Abbot, where she had arranged to meet Eddy later that evening. And, in order to meet Eddy, she had to make excuses to the boy from Sealhayne College, because he, too, had wanted to see her that evening.

That evening she went to Goodrington with Eddy. Frank Andrews and his girl were with them. The two pairs separated. Eddy was quiet. Vera sat up beside him on the high sea wall. Eddy asked Vera where she had been that afternoon.

"Seeing my grandmother," Vera said.

"You frizzy-haired, lying bugger!" Eddy gave her a wallop, which sent her flying off the wall. She landed in the sand with her legs sticking up in the air.

From then on Vera took Eddy more seriously.

Eddy began to sleep weekends at the Palk Arms. He was put on the spooky top floor, the one without lights.

Eddy did not meet with Ned's approval. When all the others had gone to bed, Eddy would hear Ned down on the middle landing mumbling to himself – saying that that bastard up there was no fucking good for his daughter, a fucking bricklayer ... Eddy would creep out of bed and jam a chair under the doorhandle.

Ned had liked Norman Weed even less.

"Big-headed little bastard," he said one day to Eddy. "I hear you gave him a hammering down the Town Hall."

"I did."

"Did 'e? I heard he threatened you with a revolver?"

"He did."

"He brought the bugger in here one night."

Eddy had heard many a tale about Ned. Most of Ellacombe and Babbacombe was afraid of him. One evening Cyril Drew, Norman Weed and a couple of others had been having a drink in the Palk Arms' back room. Ned had come in, had rolled up his sleeves.

"Span my wrist," he said to Cyril. Cyril Drew was a plumber. Ned had wrists as thick as pork hams.

"Biggest wrist in Torquay, Mr Avery," Cyril said, winking at the others to humour him.

"Span my wrist," Ned said to the next.

"Can't get nowhere near it, Mr Avery. Never seen a wrist like it."

Ned came to Norman Weed.

"Span my wrist," Ned said.

"Not bad," Norman said. Ned hit him on the forehead with the flat of his hand. Norman's grey trilby hat crumpled up and Norman slid unconscious under the table.

Ned liked horses, cards, drink, ferreting and dirty jokes. But he did not tell dirty jokes; and neither did he swear in front of women, nor allow any other man to do so. In the Palk Arms, the women drank in the secluded 'snug' room, away from the men.

A man at Babbacombe regatta had said something rude to Vera's mother by way of a joke. Ned had hurt him so bad the man had been unconscious for three days.

Yet, every year at Torquay regatta, it was Ned who paid for all the children from St Vincent's Orphanage and for all the boys from the Brixham Seaman's Orphanage, for one ride each on every roundabout and on the helter-skelter slide.

Vera arranged for Eddy to become a lodger at Mrs Dredge's, just up the road from the Palk Arms.

Mrs Dredge had two boys, a daughter, and three other lodgers. One lodger was a newspaper reporter; then there was Harry, and a man from the Post Office. They all slept in one large room upstairs, like a dormitory, and they all paid one pound and ten shillings a week.

Eddy now saw much more of Vera. Rene and Cyril Perry borrowed a car and took Vera and Eddy to Plymouth for the day. On the way back, they stopped the car and Vera and Eddy took a rug up into a dark field for a cuddle. When they got back into the car, Rene asked what the awful smell was. In the light of the Palk Arms, they saw that Vera had lain in some cow muck. Vera rushed upstairs for a bath.

Most of Ellacombe were Vera's customers. Eddy could not stop to talk to a girl without Vera finding out about it. On a seat on Ellacombe green, Eddy asked Vera to become engaged to him. Vera agreed.

Eddy had to ask Ned's permission. Generally, there was a game of cards going on in the middle room – police and publicans – to all hours of the night. This night, after official closing, Eddy said: "I want to speak to you, Dad."

"What you want? Better come out into the yard."

Eddy thought, *Christ* – that was where Ned took the wayward customers and belted them from one wall to the next.

"I want to get married to Babe," Eddy said.

"I don't know about that," Ned said, and he walked up the yard shaking his head. Eddy walked with him.

"You're only a bricklayer. You ain't got no prospects. And we've spent all this money on her, put Babe into business over there." *You haven't spent any money,* Eddy thought. It was her mother's money. And up and down the yard they went. For an hour and a half.

Vera and her mother had crept into the pantry, which had a window opening onto the yard. The pantry was as big as a room, had whole cheeses, hams and chests of tea stacked on its shelves.

"How much you earning?" Ned asked. "I've got a lovely daughter and I expect the best for her." Vera and her mother listened in a sweat.

" 'Course," Ned added, "I likes you better than that other one she had. But I don't know." Again, Ned shook his head.

Eddy was fed up. When they again neared the back gate Eddy stood his distance and said: "Well it don't make a bit of difference if you say yes or no. I'm only asking you, but I'm getting engaged tomorrow whatever you say." Eddy knew that he could have cleared the gate and easily outdistanced him if Ned had taken a swing at him.

"Oh yes. Well ..." and to Eddy's consternation Ned began to cry. "My little maid. My little darling. That's alright boy. You'm after me own heart. I'll give you my blessings. My sonny."

When the two men got back indoors, the women were as white as sheets. Ned sent them up to bed.

"We had better have a drink on this," Ned announced to Eddy.

Eddy was drunk for three days.

Two

Pre-War: Engagement, Wedding & Marriage

Vera's mother said that she could have an engagement party or money. Vera chose to have a party in the large room above the Tudor Tea Rooms in St Marychurch.

Eddy's Granny Gill came down from Chudleigh. Eddy's friends were playing in the band. All was swinging.

Half past ten, five taxis arrived with all the boozers from the Palk Arms. Ned bought everyone drinks. The dance band ended up on the floor. One of the band was a policeman. He had a motorbike, but he was so drunk he couldn't even get on it.

Eddy Coraline danced with Vera.

"Here you!" Granny Gill shouted at him. "Clear off! Dancing with Eddy's girl. He won't like that. You'll get a hammering. Clear off!"

Eddy Coraline, who was much bigger than Eddy, said to him: "Your Gran's as bad as you."

Vera took on an apprentice to help her in the shop. Most of her customers were working women, came to the shop in their overalls, confided in her about their love affairs, their husbands, their children. Business grew.

She had started with two cubicles and a waiting room downstairs. The rest of the place was let to a family – the downstairs backroom being their sitting room. Vera hired it off them, put in another cubicle. Still it wasn't enough. So when the family moved out she took over their flat, put four more cubicles upstairs. But the bigger she got, the less money she made because the more customers she had, the more people she had to employ. In the end she had Rene, Eileen, Margaret, Margery and Phil working for her.

Ron, Margaret Cornelia's husband, and Cyril Perry and Eddy would call at the shop to wait for the girls, who didn't usually finish until gone six. Cyril Perry drove a removal van. Sitting in the back of the shop they listened to the women talking; and the talk was dirtier than that of men on building sites.

Rene and Cyril, like Eddy and Vera, were engaged. Herb, Rene's brother, and Doll, Vera's sister, were married. So, with Herb and Doll acting as chaperones, the six of them rented a caravan above Hele village, stayed there every summer weekend.

Friday nights, Doll drove them up in Ned's car, a Standard Nine. The three girls slept in the caravan. The three men slept in a tent beside it. The summer was hot.

Vera and Rene had to work late Friday evenings – until the last customer had gone. So, too, did Doll and Herb. Herb was the manager of the Co-op grocery department. Doll helped out in the Palk Arms. Eddy and Cyril finished earlier.

One Friday, rather than hang about at the caravan, Eddy and Cyril went for a drink in the Standard in Hele village. A game of darts in the public bar ended when Eddy stuck one in an old man's backside. They moved to the lounge. Cyril led the sing-song. He had a good voice, sang 'Laugh Clown Laugh' and 'The Road to Mandalay'. Eddy joined in 'Just A Song at Twilight'. Eddy couldn't sing. Nor was he as drunk as Cyril.

When they finally made their way up to the caravan, Cyril kept walking up the sides of the hedges in the lane.

"Isn't this bloody road awkward?" Cyril said.

"What you doin' of, Cyril?" Eddy asked him.

"What you think I'm doing?" Cyril said. "I'm walking."

Back at the caravan Eddy put Cyril's head under a pump. It made no difference. Eddy propped Cyril beside the door inside the caravan. The Standard Nine arrived. They'd brought a chip supper with them. Herb was a teetotaller. He came bouncing into the caravan. But no sooner did he shout: "Here's fish and chips, boys!" than Cyril threw up.

The caravan was splattered with vomit. Rene promptly gave Cyril back his engagement ring. The rest were just as angry. Eddy talked nine to the dozen to try to cover up for both of them. But the weekend was a dead loss. Next day, Vera fell out with Eddy, gave him back his engagement ring. That put Eddy in a temper. He started back along the Newton road. The rest packed everything into the car and drove after Eddy. Herb pulled up alongside him.

"Come on, Eddy. Get on in."

"No," Eddy said. "Bugger her! And the bloody car as well!"

They left him there. Eddy shouted after them to stick their car up their jacksies. Vera arrived home to a mystery never to be explained. Eddy was in the kitchen of the Palk Arms drinking tea. He had been so mad he couldn't remember how he had got there.

That summer Vera and Rene often fell out with Eddy and Cyril – if not because of their drinking then because of their gambling. Herb and Doll liked to gamble too. Most hot days, Cyril, Eddy, Herb and Doll were shut up inside the boiling caravan while Vera and Rene, left with nothing else to do and wishing that they'd all gone to the beach or for a walk, crept instead around the nearby fields spying on the courting couples, seeing how many they could catch doing it.

One afternoon, Cyril lost his week's wages, his rent money, even his radio. By six that night he'd won it all back.

Other afternoons the men and the girls separated for a nap. One afternoon the girls were woken by screaming and yelling. They looked out the caravan window. Eddy was stark naked, kept scrambling up to the tent and being thrown out again.

The three men slept on one mattress in the tent. Cyril and Herb had awoken sweating and had searched for the cause of the heat.

"It's you Darto."

Eddy had gone to bed with his long plus-four socks on. So Cyril and Herb had stripped him, had thrown him out and had refused to let him back in. Eddy had to try to fight his way back into the tent at the same time as keeping his nakedness covered

Eddy bumped into Norman Weed in Ellacombe Post Office. Both of them were buying Vera a birthday card. Solemnly they shook hands.

The caravan was rented from the farmer, Bill Clemens, for a shilling and sixpence a week – that would buy you half a box of matches these days. Bill Clemens was a miserable sod, had a lie-in on Sunday mornings – didn't get up until half-past-six. And he had a son who dalked drough 'is dose. Cyril and Eddy loathed him. Though they did offer to help him with the haymaking.

Cyril and Eddy did the pitching. The boy did the driving. They were given as much scrumpy cider as they could drink. Traditionally the farmer gave the harvesters a good tea as well. Bill Clemens didn't. He was too mean. Eddy said to Cyril: "Wish we could have a drive of this bloody horse."

Cyril said to the boy: "Here, let's have the reins."

"Dow," the boy said. "By dad wouldn't let 'e."

"Don't be so bloody mean," Cyril said.

"Dell by fadder ob you."

"Garn," Cyril said. "Let's have a drive of the horse."

"You idn't goin' dribe by horse."

"Oh get out the bloody way." Cyril shoved the boy arse-over-tit into the hay, grabbed up the reins and walloped the horse.

The horse took off, raced across the field, losing its load of hay, with Eddy and Cyril and the boy hanging on for dear life.

Grumpy before the haymaking, after it Clemens became dumb. To avoid him they had to creep down to the lavatory in the farmyard. The lavatory had a wooden seat and a different magazine every week for toilet paper. One morning Eddy returned from the lavatory furious – he'd been following a serial and somebody had ripped out the pages for arse-wipe before he'd got there.

Another day Eddy's head appeared above the bushes at the top of the field.

"Herb! Cyril!" He waved his arm, urgently beckoning them, "Herb! Cyril!" They ran up to him.

"What's happened?" they asked.

"I've shit meself," Eddy said. Herb and Cyril weren't that surprised – they'd put Epsom Salts in his tea. Eddy hadn't been able to get his trousers down in time.

From that day on, their catchphrase, wherever they were, became a huge beckoning arm and a hoarse: "Herb! Cyril!"

One morning – the girls in the caravan, the men in their tent – they all awoke and each one thought they were hearing things. Outside were people speaking French and German. Cautiously they peered out. A little French boy was balancing on a big man's hand.

Bertram Mills Circus had arrived.

In the night, without waking one of them, the entire circus had parked their caravans and pitched their tents. The caravans would be kept up in Hele, the Big Top down the town.

Doll and Herb, Vera and Eddy, Rene and Cyril spent the day watching the goings on, were fascinated by a five-year-old French boy learning his father's trade of tightrope walking. The five-year-old boy was as fascinated by their card games.

More beautiful black-haired children practised on a trapeze. One of those dark-haired, dark-eyed boys took a gun and shot all of Clemens' chickens. And the morning the circus left, Bill

Clemens was up at four to sit at the gate of the field with his shotgun – in case the circus tried to get away without paying.

Mornings, they took turns to fry the breakfast over an open fire – four rashers of bacon each and as many eggs as they wanted. One Sunday evening Vera was washing the day's dirty dishes. It was raining.

Vera squatted beside the hissing fire with a raincoat over her head, listening to the others talking inside the caravan. Not one of them offered to help, made matters worse by laughing at her efforts from within the dry caravan. Cyril added fuel to her fire by teasing her – poking his head out of the window to ask how much longer she'd be.

Vera steamed. Cyril poked his head out yet again to tell her to get a move on. Vera had the washing-up bowl in her hands. She turned and threw the water.

But Cyril had gone back in and Eddy had looked out to see how she was doing. He'd just had a wash and shave and had put on a clean shirt. The washing up water hit him full in the face. He looked at her amazed. "What'd I do?"

Doll and Herb, and Vera and Eddy, went up to Blackpool for a week. One evening they went to the Shilling Theatre. The theatre was long and narrow with the audience seated to one side of the aisle and the orchestra to the other, with the stage below. That evening there was a talent contest. It was won by Tessie O'Shea and Donald Piers.

On Boxing Night, after drinking all afternoon, they went to the Town Hall. Cyril and Eddy had a big cigar each. Eddy had on a brand new grey suit. They were full of booze. Eddy's father was at the dance. He looked like Eddy except that he was shorter and blockier. He and Ned had been drinking together all day.

Eddy was told that his father was in a bit of trouble in the bar. Eddy found him and asked what the trouble was.

"I met this young lady," his father said. "And I picked up her handbag. And that man said that I shouldn't have picked up her handbag. So I put him out. And that's that." Eddy let him get on with his drinking.

Cyril walked straight off the edge of the stage. The stage was three-foot-six high. Cyril didn't hurt himself. What with the cigar and booze Eddy didn't feel so good. He locked himself in the lavatory. He had diarrhoea, was sick on his new suit. People kept banging on the door for him to come out. Eddy wouldn't. They fetched Arthur Palmer. Arthur Palmer was a hard case. Eddy opened the door enough to see him, and belted him. Cyril was left to face Arthur Palmer.

When the dance was over, they got Eddy into a taxi and up to Mrs Dredge's. He sat in the middle of the road. Cyril tried to pull him to his feet.

Eddy hit Cyril.

"You bastard!" Cyril said.

"What will Missus Dredge think of me?" Eddy said.

"If you don't go in I'm finishing with you," Vera said.

"Well bloody well finish with me," Eddy said.

Cyril and Vera knocked on Mrs Dredge's door. Aunty answered it. Aunty liked chaps. She fetched all the men down from the dormitory and they carried Eddy up the three stories to bed.

Eddy's father had stayed for Christmas at Mrs Dredge's. When Eddy came to, he thought he'd better go downstairs and see how his father was. He wasn't there. Eddy started to walk down to the Palk Arms, met his father coming home.

His father had gone to meet the young lady in the Town Hall and had gone through the wrong door. He had got lost and spent the night wandering around the empty council offices. The caretaker let him out when he unlocked the place in the morning. Now his father couldn't shave for trembling. He said it was due to the malaria he had caught while serving out East during the Great War.

Eddy was working for Narracott. Narracott was a friend of Ned's. Ned was a director of Torquay United Football Club. Narracott was also a director of Torquay United. Ned and Narracott would be in the inside room playing cards and drinking whisky with the local police inspectors and detectives until three in the morning. The police station was only down the road in Market Street.

Eddy didn't like working for the Narracotts. There were too many yes-men on the firm. To keep the job they almost had to kiss the boss's arse. The bricklayers weren't allowed to smoke.

Eddy didn't have overalls when he started on the site. He had been working away, had only brown boots and trousers. As a test, Eddy was put to work against Narracott's foreman, Stanley. Eddy could have slaughtered him as far as speed was concerned. But Stanley started off fast. So Eddy decided to give him a run for his money.

They were laying blocks. Stanley hadn't laid blocks before. Eddy had. Soon Eddy was ahead of him and Stanley's wall was bellying.

Bob Narracott came up to them. He stood with his hands behind his back. A gold watch chain was stretched across his belly. Jimmy Narracott stood behind him.

"What's the matter with your hand son?" Bob Narracott said to Eddy. Eddy looked over his hands for a cut.

"I don't mean a cut," Bob Narracott said. "I mean the bloody gold ring there. Gold ring. No uniform. Brown boots. What's it comin' to?"

"All you want to be concerned about," Eddy said, "is my bloody work. Anyhow, you're only an old stonemason, and you've got a gold ring and a gold watch chain."

"You mustn't talk to my father like that," Jimmy Narracott said.

"Piss off," Eddy said. "I've had trouble with you before. I'm doing half the bloody work on this wall."

"I know that. I know that," Bob Narracott said.

"You want to be more concerned with my work than with what I'm wearing."

Bob Narracott went to stand at the end of the wall. From there he could see the foreman's wall.

"Stanley," Bob Narracott said, "if that cavity gets any bigger down your end I'll be able to sit in the bloody thing." And that put Eddy right in it with the foreman. Thereafter, when it was raining, Eddy would be the only one outside still working while everyone else was in the shed, dry.

Jimmy Narracott was a very good skater. He had once been out with a girl of Eddy's. There'd been a bit of a fuss. On the site, though, the bricklayers had to call the boss's son 'Master'.

"You haven't got that chimney breast right," Jimmy said to Eddy on one site.

"What've I got to do different then?" Eddy asked him. The other brickies were all listening.

"You haven't got the vents in," Jimmy said.

"What d'you mean, the vents?"

"You can understand a plan?" Jimmy asked him.

"I spent four years in an architect's office," Eddy said. " 'Course I can understand a bloody plan."

"Well what about the vents?"

"Bloody vents," Eddy said. "That's the flue you silly bugger."

"You're supposed to call me 'Master Jim'."

Because of all that, Eddy didn't want any special favours from Narracott just because he was about to become Ned's son-in-law. Not telling him who he was marrying, Eddy asked Stanley for a week's holiday for his honeymoon. Stanley said that he couldn't have a holiday. Eddy said that he was taking it anyway.

The day of the wedding Eddy wasn't allowed in the Palk Arms. Not that he wanted to – he had to go down the Spa for a massage to slap him back into shape after the stag night. Then he had to go and have a plate of five new teeth fitted. Their newness made him retch.

The other men gathered in the Palk Arms before the ceremony. Shortly after opening time a man came in.

"Pint please."

"Haven't seen you in here before," Ned said.

"No," the man said. "But I heard you had some good beer so I come in for a pint."

"Well that one's on the house," Ned said. "My daughter's getting married today."

The man downed the pint, said thank you and good morning. And, throughout the day, strange men came in, one after the other, for their free pint.

The ceremony was in Ellacombe Church. Most of the men were drunk by the time of the service. Ned stood on Vera's veil, tore it in half. The usual vicar hadn't been able to make it: an old vicar performed the service. He didn't approve of Vera's ring, kept staring at it, breaking off the service and going back to the beginning again.

"How much bloody longer?" Ned asked – he thought he was whispering. "I'll never get up."

Eddy retched, thought, *how the hell did I get here?* He had never intended getting married – events seemed to have overtaken him. *Ah well,* he thought, *too late now.*

After the ceremony the guests continued to drink. Later in the afternoon Cyril Blackler and the rest staggered over to the Empire Cinema, had a sleep, and then started again. By nine thirty the Palk Arms was dry.

By that time Vera and Eddy were well on their way to Bournemouth. Vera had worn a black beret with a belted white coat to go off on her honeymoon. And while they were on honeymoon she wouldn't let Eddy have a little bit in a bathing hut because that day she had toothache.

Vera and Eddy had paid fifty pounds deposit for a house in Congella Road. It was a steep road just below a copse of cedars. Doll and Herb had a house in Pine View Road about two hundred yards below them.

Vera and Eddy had bought the house from Fred White, a friend of Ned's. They used their own money. Eddy had saved it playing seven nights a week in the band, was pleased to, at last, have a house of his own, after having lived in digs for so long.

Eddy couldn't have saved the money bricklaying. Bricklayers were two a penny. The only work was hotel extensions; and the hotels were busy in the summer. Bricklayers would be taken on for a day or two, then sacked.

In Congella Road, as man and wife, Vera packed up Eddy's sandwiches for the first time and sent him off to work. An hour later Eddy was back with his bike and all his tools. He had gone to get up on the lorry to Maidencombe, where they'd been building some bungalows, and Stanley had said that Eddy's tools were back at the yard; he was sacked. He was paid the one day he was owed, and that was that.

Ned found out.

"Wait till I see bloody Narracott," he said, and went straight to him.

"You're a fine bloody pal," Ned told him, "sacking my son-in-law." Narracott didn't know what Ned was talking about. Ned told him the story.

"I never knew he was your son-in-law," Narracott said. "Tell the bugger to come back." But Eddy wouldn't go back to work for him, got himself a job with Vanstone instead. Vanstone was another director of Torquay United FC.

Fred Bryce-Rundell was a foreman on Vanstone's. He was a right bastard. One labourer in particular he always picked on. The labourer had eight children, worked like a donkey. Bryce-Rundell took a delight in threatening him with the sack and making him cry.

Fred Bryce-Rundell could only spell one word. That one word being 'Fred'. And, that being the one word he was confident with, he called all the men working for him Fred. So, when he shouted, "Fred!" everyone on the site had to stop work and look around to see who he meant.

He'd been in trouble for indecent language when they built the Regal in Castle Circus. He was fined four pounds. A Cockney bricklayer tried to kill him on that job, had picked up a brick, held it endwise and dropped it. But it missed Bryce-Rundell's head and only skimmed his shoulder.

There was an Irish carpenter on the Torquay Grammar School job. Every so often he would have a funny turn. He had one on that job, chased Bryce-Rundell down all the corridors of the school with an axe; and, when Bryce-Rundell locked himself in a shed, the Irishman started to chop down the door. They took the Irishman away in a straitjacket.

The boss, though, liked Bryce-Rundell. He pushed a job. Eddy worked with him on the library beside the Town Hall – on the grassy patch where Eddy had fought Norman Weed. Downstairs in the library they had to build a big passageway. They were using a new sort of block – six feet long and very light, made of some kind of straw. It needed two bricklayers to get them to the line. But they were easy to lay, as they didn't shake.

"I want this up," Bryce-Rundell said.

The brickies put their heads together. First they built all the side walls out as far as they would go, then they whacked the passage up. The scaffolding was thrown over and the inside walls finished.

At about four o'clock Bryce-Rundell came around.

"Bloody hell, Fred," he said. "You haven't half got on well here."

One of the brickies, Dick, looked at what they had done.

"Where's the doors?" he said.

"What doors?"

"To get into all the rooms."

"You never said nothing about doors," one of the brickies said to Bryce-Rundell.

"You should know there'd be doors down there," Bryce-Rundell said.

"Bloody ignorant we are. Bricklayers," the brickie said. "We don't know nothing." They had to saw the doors out of the blocks to put the jambs in.

Ned got taken ill with his kidneys. Eddy sat with him. Vera's mother said that Eddy was the only man who could do anything with him. Dr Wall ordered Ned to bed for four days. As soon as Dr Wall was gone Ned leant across to Eddy.

"That old cunt."

"What'd you say, Ned?"

"I said that old cunt be gone before me."

Next morning when Dr Wall called, Ned was in the cellar chucking about hogsheads of beer.

Now that Vera had made a go of the shop, Lewish the landlord said that he wanted it for his own hairdressing shop. Vera's parents loaned her the money to buy the shop from him. She paid them back week by week.

Eddy played in Frank's band at Broadhempston fete. They played in the field in the afternoon, then down at the village hall in the evening. Mosley's Fascist Brownshirts came that evening on a recruiting drive. All they got from the local farmboys were bruises. The same as when they'd gone to Torquay – where the Brownshirts had been given a hell of a hiding outside Woolworth's.

Up until then Frank's band had worn black shirts – specially made – and had worn red ties with them. After receiving a few too many threats they gave up wearing them, wore blue Russian smock shirts instead.

As well as Cyril and Rene and Herb and Doll, there was now a whole crowd of recently married couples who got together at weekends. Apart from the four girls who worked with Vera – and their fiancées and husbands – there was Betty and Cyril Blackler, Eileen and Les, Margaret and Ron, Vera and Len Toms, Eddy and Nora, Doris and Des, and Doris and Bert Rook. Most Saturdays they went to dances together; but at Christmas they each gave a party, weekend after weekend, all putting into the pot for the booze.

At Vera's party in Congella Road that Christmas, Betty was nine months pregnant, and huge. Cyril Drew and Eddy decided to bring the baby along. They laid Betty on a table, covered her with a sheet, and from under the sheet they took – one by one – a doll, a string of sausages, a glass eye ...

"Oh. Here's a set of jugs." Betty laughed so much that she peed all over the table. Two days later she gave birth.

The mainstay of their weekends was Vera Toms. She was a blonde as big as Tessie O'Shea, light as a feather on her feet, and could mix with anyone rich or poor, crack her jaw with the best of them – go from the Chief Constable of Devon on her table and talk to the navvy on the next. She was the manageress of a posh restaurant called The Epicure in Torwood Street.

Most weekends the crowd of them started off in The Gibbons, where Vera and Rene had a Pimms No 1 each; and Cyril and Eddy grumbled at the price of a shilling and two pence. Then they all trooped over to the Pavilion. Clarkes & Rowe put on a different variety show there each week. Tommy Fields, Gracie Fields' brother, was there.

After the Pavilion they went up to The Epicure for a free dinner. And after dinner they all went back to Vera Toms' house in Scarborough Terrace, off Belgrave Road. Often the theatre crowd would go with them – Rupert Rogers included. It was a big house: Nora and Eddy shared it with Vera and Len.

New Year's Eve, Vera Toms gave a party. Beforehand Vera let it be known that, at great expense, she had a treat in store for them. Vera knew that Eddy and Cyril had been going up to the house on the quiet, and that Vera Toms had been to Beard's, the most expensive hairdressers, and had hired wigs.

New Year's Eve, Vera Toms announced them, and on they trouped like chorus girls. Vera Toms being big, the two Eddies, Cyril, Len and Des had all dressed in her evening gowns. And their rehearsals had made them immaculate in their high stepping. The joke was well appreciated, especially as every time the men kicked up their legs their baggy underpants revealed their all.

Some weekends the crowd of married couples crammed into their few cars and went over to Broadsands. Vera and Rene and Cyril and Betty Blackler would stay in the warm sea for up to four or five hours at a time while all the others sat behind the bushes playing cards.

Some weekends they went to Goodrington. There they hired two beach huts. Ned and Vera's mother came over between pub opening times; and, while Vera and Rene lay in the sun, the rest crowded into one of the beach huts and gambled away the day.

Like Churchill, Eddy could see that a war was coming. He said as much to Ned. Ned called Eddy a Nazi.

At that time they used to have crazy dances. Men would arrive with their shirts on backwards and with their ties down their backs.

The bandleader would say: "Take your partners for a waltz." And the band would play a Charleston. The other Eddy, Cyril and the rest used to go as a rugby club. Little Horace was used as the ball.

Eddy was playing in the band at one dance. He came off the drums to join in. They had practised. Mendelssohn's Spring Song was played on the piano. They had a tea chest covered with a tablecloth, with some flowers on top. Out of the tea chest they lifted little, fat Horace. Then they threw him from one to the other. He had on red tights with a hole in each cheek. Every time they picked him up his hairy arse stuck out.

One night Eddy and Cyril, with an arm and a leg each, were swinging Horace around. He was heavy. He slipped out of their hands and slid across the dance floor until a wall stopped him. The audience thought it was part of the act. The routine became such a success that, on the strength of it, they were invited to perform at the Midnight Matinee, a big charity event. And, after that, many more.

On October 1st 1938 Chamberlain returned from Munich with his piece of paper. Vera and Eddy thought, *Thank God for that,* and breathed a sigh of relief.

At a party in Vera Toms' house they played sardines. Eddy had on a new suit. He went upstairs first and hid under a bed. Vera Toms went next, got under the bed with Eddy. The next one to go under was Cyril. Come the end there must have been fifteen people under that bed, packed so tight that the bed was off the floor. Vera Toms laughed so much she wet herself; and, being a big woman, she swamped Eddy and Cyril.

Another night Vera and Eddy met a man in a pub, invited him along to the Co-op Social. He was a tall man, talked like Mr Christian in Mutiny On The Bounty.

In the dance Eddy said: "Ah, here comes Mr Christian." The other Eddy laughed so much that his false teeth – he'd had them young – shot out, top and bottom set, and slid across the slippery dance floor.

"Shtop my bloody sheesh!" Eddy shouted.

Another night Vera Toms had been working late and arrived at the party with a man wearing a monocle. He was thin, had a big nose. They all wondered who the hell Vera had got hold of now.

"I felt so sorry for this poor man," Vera Toms said. "He came in to have a meal, doesn't know a soul here, so I've brought him along. This is Algernon. Algie." He looked like a parrot, but he had a lovely time.

One night, at a party in Scarborough Terrace, Vera Toms came over to Vera, asked if she knew another couple there. Neither Vera nor Rene knew them.

"Excuse me dear," Vera Toms said as she stopped by the couple, "but do I know you?"

"Well … no," the woman answered, "but you all seemed to be having such a good time in the pub," (they had been in the Victoria and Albert) "that we just followed you."

"Oh you're very welcome," Vera Toms told them.

After a while Cyril showed the new couple Vera Toms' Indian carpet. It looked just like an ordinary carpet. But if you looked at it long enough you could see, all over it, pairs of dogs and sheep mounting one another.

On New Year's Eve they always had a table for thirty at 'The 400', got a discount because they livened the place up, got the dance going. Vera Toms was without doubt the star, very popular, all nineteen-stone of her – two hundred and sixty-six pounds of woman on the hoof. She had a thigh like a side of beef.

That night they played musical chairs – the girl having to sit on the man's lap when the music stopped. Vera Toms and another couple, strangers to them, were left with the last chair to fight over. It being New Year's Eve, there was a good prize for the winners. When the music stopped Eddy went to sit on the chair but the other man yanked it from under him. Eddy went down with all nineteen stones of Vera Toms on top of him.

When Eddy got his wind back, which took some time, he was furious. "That was a bloody silly thing to do," he told the man.

"What're you going to do about it?" the man said. Eddy could see he was looking for trouble.

"I'll soon bloody ..." Eddy began, but Vera Toms pushed Eddy aside with one hand and punched the man with the other. The man went down and out.

They fanned him, gave him brandy; and when he came round Len Toms said to him: "If I were you, I'd go. I don't like blokes fighting with my wife. So if you don't piss off quick you'll get the hammering of your life."

The man was hardly conscious, but managed to say: "If you're anything like your missus, I'm off."

Walking home from the dance they passed by the police station in Market Street. They were singing. A new young policeman, just down from the Police College in Exeter, shouted out to them: "Less bloody row!"

They all stopped.

"Row? What d'you mean – row?" Len said. "We were singing."

"You're not allowed to do that."

"And who's going to stop us?" Len asked him. "Bloody little kid like you?" Len turned to the others. "Let's go in the station and sort 'em out." They all started for the station door.

The Sergeant came out laughing. "Get on home, Len. And you buggers. The boy don't know no different."

The crowd of them went for Sunday walks – down the Teign valley, over the moors to Lustleigh. Eddy took them all up to Lord Clifford's estate at Chudleigh. He took them on the only day of the year when the estate was closed. He had earned his title of Guide Dart.

Another time they were supposed to be going to a river. Guide Dart led them up a steep hill crowned with trees.

"Well, Guide Dart," Cyril said. "I may be wrong, but if you're following a river, what the bloody hell are we doing up here?"

Ned retired, left the Palk Arms, and moved into a house in Congella – two doors along from Vera and Eddy, with Mac's house in between.

A German spy was caught in St Marychurch. He was well known locally, did watercolours of the landscape, mostly cliffs. The lady he lodged with noticed that he often sent tins of Tucker's toffees to Holland. One night the landlady's husband happened to go into the painter's room, couldn't figure out what was causing a musty smell.

In one of the cupboards he saw that the floorboards were loose. He lifted them out and found underneath thousands of mouldy Tucker's toffees. What the painter had been doing had been making drawings all around the coast – especially of Plymouth and Start Point – then tipping the contents out of a tin of Tucker's toffees, stuffing his drawings into the bottom, covering them with toffees and sending the tin to his contact in Holland.

Some Sunday mornings the crowd of them left at seven to go up to Ethel's at Mortenhempstead. Ethel would have breakfast awaiting them, gave them lunch and tea. They all paid her.

Ethel's husband, Billy, took them for what he called a one-mile walk – more like seven – from Drogo Castle to Fingal Bridge. Once they had to run the whole way because of swarms of flying ants.

Sometimes they stayed the whole weekend. It was so crowded then that Vera and Rene had to sleep under the kitchen table. During the days they went swaling; and, when there was snow, tobogganing.

Ethel was tall. Billy was a little short-arse. He had a whippet dog. When Billy got drunk – regularly – Ethel carried him home from the pub. Sober, though, Billy had a nose for nature. On a Sunday morning walk he'd stop beside a hole.

"Hang on a minute boys. There's a bloody fox having a yek in there." He was rarely wrong.

Billy was drunk the day they went swaling. He fell over and set fire to a plantation of trees just below Fingal Bridge. The rest of them managed to put it out.

A Mortenhempstead simpleton followed Vera and Rene wherever they went.

"I likes you two," he said. Old Fuzz they called him.

In the evenings they played cards.

Ethel's brother, Ernie, was a terror for the women. He was a first class granite mason, worked for two firms in London. Any job requiring granite, they sent for him; and the job could take anything up to five months. One day Eddy went to watch him at work in Blackdown quarry. Ernie split up a block of granite, no trouble at all. He cut the granite for the Houses of Parliament. And in whatever digs Ernie stayed, he shacked up with the landlady.

Ernie's wife, Fanny, was very ladylike, very plain, and very prim. She was a schoolteacher.

They played Pontoon, and whenever Fanny said: "I'm sticking,"

Vera said: "Fanny's sticking."

Rene said, "Fanny's sticking."
Eddy said, "Fanny's sticking."
And Cyril said, "Fanny's sticking."
And Fanny was so prim and proper that she never saw the joke.

Three

September 3rd 1939 – April 8th 1940

September 3rd 1939: War declared. 'Athenia' torpedoed and sunk.

September 17th 1939: Russian armies enter Poland. (Partitioned between Germany and Russia).

October 14th 1939: 'Royal Oak' torpedoed in Scapa Flow.

October 21st 1939: Registration of all men for call-up begins. Four divisions of B.E.F. (British Expeditionary Force) on Franco-Belgian border.

November 8th 1939: Georg Elser puts a time bomb under Hitler's rostrum. Hitler leaves early. Seven people killed.

December 1939: Luftwaffe bombing British fishermen in North Sea. 'Graf Spee' rounded up by Royal Navy.

January 1940: Hard winter. One million unemployed.

January 8th 1940: Rationing began. Chunking bombed by Japanese air force.

February 1940: British prisoners rescued from 'Attmark'.

March 1940: Six more divisions of B.E.F. sent to Franco-Belgian border.

March 12th 1940: Finns defeated by Russians.

April 4th 1940: Chamberlain declares that the Germans "... have missed the bus."

September 3rd 1939 was a Sunday. Vera and Eddy went two doors along for lunch at her mother and father's. They all knew that war was about to be declared. They waited by the radio. At eleven, Chamberlain announced: "We are now at war with Germany ..."

Ned was a great supporter of the Royal Navy, the Senior Service. In the Great War, he had volunteered for the Navy, only to be turned down because of his fatty heart.

"No-one'll get past the Royal Navy," he said. Later that day they heard that the SS Athenia had been sunk.

Eddy was building some council houses at Coombe Pafford. Luckily, they were almost finished, because – at the end of that week – all the jobs stopped. The site kept on two plasterers to finish off those houses already built, and one bricklayer, Jack Marlin, to clear up any odds and ends. But Eddy was out of work.

No-one was allowed to trawl. So Eddy went fishing down at Long Quarry every day, catching pollock and selling them to Cann's, the fishmongers.

Three weeks after war had been declared, Vera was at Long Quarry with him, along with Tom Cox and his wife. It was a calm day. They were catching mackerel. A big black plane was flying around. Tom Cox looked at it.

"Here!" he said. "That's a bloody Dornier. A flying pencil. That's a bastard Jerry!" Charley Hibbs was there. He was a bricklayer. So was Eli Mannen.

"He's right you know," Charley Hibbs said. The papers encouraged the public to spot planes.

They watched the plane circle Long Quarry, then the Nose. Then he went over and dropped his bombs just off Teignmouth pier. Eddy went home and told Ned. After that, Ned did not sleep. Night after night he walked up and down his back garden listening for any planes coming over and calling them all the names under the sun, and bellowing at people to cover up their lights.

All the men decided to volunteer. They had a big supper and told their wives they were all going out for a drink together. The women went up to Vera's.

The drill hall was in Rock Road, behind Abbey Road. The men met at Castle Circus. They went first for a drink in the Castle. From the Castle they went to the White Hart. From the White Hart they went to the Banner Cross. Then they went to the Prince of Wales, the Exeter and the Forresters. They then decided that the drill hall would be closed if they didn't go back soon. So they doubled back up to Rock Road.

Cyril Blackler, being a plumber, was the only one they could take. Cyril Drew, the other plumber, had a perforated eardrum. And all the rest were in reserved occupations. Frank was a carpenter, Eddy a bricklayer. If Eddy could have got in then, they told him, he could have gone straight in as a Staff Sergeant in charge of maintenance on aerodromes. But on Eddy's employment card was a certain number and no-one was allowed to alter that number, and that meant that he had to wait until he was called up.

By the time they left Rock Road, they were all very drunk, and downcast. On the way home, they had to pass Herb's grocers shop in Ellacombe. A teetotaller, he smiled as he watched the brave lads stagger past. When Eddy got home, he collapsed.

Evacuees began to arrive from London. Haldon pier was still open. Three evacuee boys came down there with the fishermen. They had a few hand-lines, were always cadging bait. One had a pair of roller skates. He would skate like the clappers along the pier, wouldn't stop until he got right to the end; and as he zipped past, he would pinch anything. He was well liked by the men, though.

Eddy talked to the three boys. Until they had been evacuated to Ellacombe, they hadn't known what a cooked meal was – apart from fish and chips.

The first people to be killed in an air raid on Torquay – in Dower Road, Upton – were two evacuees.

When the Courageous was torpedoed in the Bristol Channel, and the Royal Oak was torpedoed in Scapa Flow, Ned was furious, swore that he'd never support the Tories again the way they'd run the Navy down so. The shock went deep for Ned: he had honestly believed that no-one would dare cross the English Channel, let alone sink the Courageous and the Royal Oak, and drop bombs on Torquay.

Eddy carried on playing in the band – for the British Legion on Saturday nights. Then he played for the RAF dance band because they didn't have a drummer. Of the others in his own band, Merv Adams was over military age, Norman Poke was deemed not fit, so too was Frank. Frank was taken on by the Prudential, who had moved their offices to Torquay. Then Frank was sent to a factory in Buckinghamshire.

Eddy tried to get into the army as a waiter, was sent instead to Torpoint to work. He had to build a brick pier to carry a bridge over a small creek. After two weeks, there was a dispute and he was sent home. He stayed home a week, then was sent to Holywell.

Holywell was fifteen miles outside Newquay. He had to help build an army camp in the sand dunes for desert training. From there, Eddy was sent to Padstow, to Treginnon aerodrome. He was bombed and strafed there several times.

All the huts on the aerodrome were being built of concrete blocks. The bricklayers came back after one raid to find nothing but heaps of rubble. The men who had the army contract for the concrete blocks had put hardly any cement in them. The Germans had dropped some bombs near the huts and the blast had turned the huts into heaps of gravel.

Everyone had to make their own blackouts. First Vera used cardboard, clipped it to the window frames. But the cardboard kept breaking. So Vera bought some heavy black cloth and tacked it over wooden frames.

Perishables were first to be rationed – meat, then butter, sugar, lard ... In the shop, hair oil was rationed. A black-market Jew offered Vera some brilliantine. She tried one bottle; but although they had dosed it with strong perfume, it still smelt of paraffin. Vera could not get any ammonia for perms and she responded to a scarcity of hairpins by purchasing bits of wire to make them herself.

Those bricklayers who were in the Territorial Army were sent from Torquay to build pillboxes on the Franco-Belgian border. Not one of them had been taught how to fire a gun. When the Germans advanced, the bricklayers were given a rifle each, some ammunition, and two grenades.

Four

April 8th 1940 – July 1940

April 8th 1940: Germans invade neutral Norway.

April 12th 1940: British troops sent to Norway. Germans beat British at Trondheim and Narvik.

May 7th 1940: Evacuation from Trondheim complete.

May 9th 1940: Germans invade Belgium and Holland.

May 13th 1940: Churchill makes his '... blood, toil, tears and sweat ... Victory at all costs ...' speech.

May 14th 1940: LDV (Local Defence Volunteers) formed. Rotterdam bombed.

May 15th 1940: Dutch beaten.

May 17th 1940: Brussels taken.

May 20th 1940: Germans reach Channel coast.

May 23rd 1940: British Fascist leader Mosley arrested. Internment of aliens begun.

May 24th 1940: B.E.F. cut off at Dunkirk.

May 26th 1940: Evacuation of Dunkirk begun.

May 27th 1940: Belgium capitulates.

May 30th 1940: Signposts removed in Britain.

June 4th 1940: Dunkirk evacuation complete. 338,226 troops taken off.

June 10th 1940: Mussolini declares war on Allies.

June 16th 1940: Reynaud resigns. Petain takes over unoccupied France.
June 18th 1940: Churchill's speech '... this their finest hour ...'
June 20th 1940: Night bombing begins.
June 22nd 1940: Armistice signed between France and Germany.
June 30th 1940: Guernsey and Jersey occupied by German forces.
July 1940: LDV renamed Home Guard. All aliens now interned.
July 18th 1940: British agree to close Burma Road.

Eddy was sent to work at Denbury army camp. Narracotts had the contract, took him up there each day in their lorry. Only Eddy and one old mason were working there. They mostly had to take down lampposts and put them in different places because the learner lorry drivers kept knocking them down. Eddy also had to brick round the open cookhouses.

Eddy had soldiers as labourers. He liked the job, was allowed to go to the NAAFI military stores and get anything he wanted. He bought all his and Vera's groceries.

While he was working there, the soldiers arrived from Dunkirk by way of Plymouth. They had no uniforms, no rifles. There were some French soldiers among them, looking bewildered. All of them looked exhausted. Eddy asked them about Dunkirk. The soldiers regarded it as a victory, had never expected a whole army to be evacuated. Some believed that if the French had stood their ground they would be fighting there still – the French outnumbered the invading Germans in both men and tanks. But the German blitzkrieg had panicked them.

Cyril Drew joined the Air Raid Patrol. Eddy joined the LDV. He went to the bank to draw his uniform. The manager was Captain Dampier. He had been an administrator in the Great War. He rode a big old-fashioned bike, lived up at Quints, above Congella.

Eddy was given a tin helmet, a pair of boots and black leggings, a hat and a denim suit. The denim suit was so baggy that he had to wear other clothes under it. The LDV had no other uniform to issue. Eddy took it all home and hung it in the wardrobe.

Mac, next door – between them and Ned – was in the auxiliary fire brigade. There had been a few tip-and-run raids that evening. Some people in Babbacombe Road had been killed. Eddy heard Mac leave. Soon after that, there was a knock on Vera and Eddy's door.

"Mr Dart live here?" a man asked.

"Yes," Eddy said.

"LDV?" the man asked.

"Yes," Eddy said.

"Report to Walls Hill rightaway. Bring all the food you can spare. The invasion's started."

Vera went into a blind panic. She only had small squares of cheese and fish. But she managed to cut Eddy a bag of sandwiches before he took her down to Ned's. Ned asked him what weapon he had. Eddy had none. Ned had a walking stick he prized – ornamented with silver.

"You take that bugger," he said and shoved it at Eddy. "And you let 'em know. Mind you bring it back though." Eddy declined it.

As Eddy came down Windsor Road to turn up Reddenhill Road, he met another man. The man asked Eddy where he was going.

"Why?" Eddy asked him. "Who are you?" They had been told to be careful who they talked to.

"I only joined the LDV yesterday," the man said.

"I only joined this evening," Eddy said.

"I'm in B Company with Corporal Bragg," the man said.

"Percy Bragg," Eddy said. "Same as me."

They walked together along Reddenhill Road until they came to the church. There were no signposts, no church bells. The iron gates and railings had all been taken away to melt down for the war effort.

"Who goes there!" a Scotsman, wearing a Tam-o'Shanter hat, challenged them. Eddy and the man showed them their LDV documents.

"Got a fag, Jock?" one of the soldiers asked them. Eddy had about thirty Woodbines on him. He gave the six soldiers on the machine gun one each.

At the bottom of St Anne's Road, on the crossroads, was another machine gun post. Eddy said goodbye to another six Woodbines. They arrived at Walls Hill. The quarry by the hut was crowded – C Company, B Company, and the Scottish boys were there. Some of the Regulars were already posted down the road to Anstey's Cove. Anstey's was mined. Redgate was not.

It was pitch dark. Eddy was told to go down to a sandbag post behind the Palace Hotel, looking down to Anstey's Cove. Before they moved off, a Brigadier from South Western Command had a word with them.

"I must make you understand that if any of you chaps are captured you will be shot out of hand. You don't come under the Regular Army. You are a guerrilla force." None of them had known that. "If they do come tonight the Regulars will have to withdraw inland to hold them. You chaps will have to do the best you can, and then withdraw to the hills and fight like guerrillas."

"What bloody hills?" Eddy said.

They then queued to be kitted out. There was an old boy in Eddy's platoon from Plainmoor, had a little white dog. He was very upright, a proper old last war bloke, and deaf as a post. He was given a rifle and twenty rounds. The rest were given ten rounds of ammo apiece, but no rifle. For weapons they were given a length of copper piping with a bayonet welded to its end.

They went to their sandbag post behind the Palace Hotel. They were just a little way up from a small stone bridge – to cover anybody who got past the two posts below them. There was a stone wall there. The old boy piled up a few stones and got himself into position, his rifle pointing down the road.

"I was in the Old Contemptibles," he said. "I could get off twenty a bloody minute." To make him understand anything they had to write it down on a piece of paper; if they tried to make him hear they had to shout so loud the Germans could have heard them across the Channel.

If the old man had been shot, the next one was supposed to take the rifle, and so on. It began to rain heavily. Not one of them had a coat. Eddy had a light mac, but that was soon soaked through. The rain bounced off their helmets. They heard a crowd march up the road past them. They couldn't see who it was through the rain. They had been told not to challenge anyone. The Old Contemptible said that it had been the patrol going back.

"That's nothing," he said.

"It may have finished," Eddy said.

"No! No! We stay here until we're relieved," the Old Contemptible said. "That's the bloody orders. And when you've got orders, orders is orders."

"Can't one of us go?" Eddy asked him. But it was hopeless; no-one could make him understand.

Daylight came. They couldn't see anyone, hear anyone. About nine o'clock, Captain Dampier came riding by on his high bike. He told them to go home. The rest had gone at one-thirty. The few German barges that had set out from across the channel had turned back.

They began training with broom handles up at Quinta. The Sergeant, Mr Truman, an ex-Sergeant Major of the Guards, lived down Lower Ellacombe Church Road. He reckoned Eddy would have made a first class Guardsman.

Jimmy Kellow, a bricklayer, sloped arms differently to the rest.

"Where did you learn that?" Mr Truman asked Jimmy. "Just how old are you for Chrissake? We haven't sloped arms like that since the Crimea."

"My granddad taught me," Jimmy said. Jimmy was seventy-six. The majority of Eddy's platoon was around that age. Most guard nights he spent watching out in case they walked over the cliffs. Jimmy Kellow did. They found his body two days later stuck in a little cave halfway down to Redgate beach.

The LDV was renamed the Home Guard. They were given real rifles and they were told that, from now on, they would be paid. As well as work, Eddy now had to do three nights' guard duty a week – from seven in the evening until eight in the morning – two hours on and two hours off.

On top of that, every Sunday they had to parade. The older ones were mustard at drill. And every Sunday when the parade was over the officer would ask the men: "Any questions?"

"Sir!" George Browning would boom out.

"Yes Browning?"

"When're the spondoolicks coming, Sir?" Their wages were three shillings a week, but it was so long before they were paid that, when they eventually received their first wage packets, they got ten pounds each.

Rene and Cyril had two evacuees from Guernsey staying with them. She was a big, jolly woman: he was small and intelligent. Vera spent most of her spare time doing crosswords, would spend a whole day puzzling over the clues, only for the Guernsey man to finish it in five minutes flat.

One day Vera found a huge spider in Rene's bathroom. She called Rene. Rene made sure that the window was open, caught the spider by one of its legs and threw it into the garden. They heard a scream, looked out to see the fat Guernsey woman running in circles around the garden and yelling that she had been stung. Her neck had a lump the size of a baby's fist on it. Neither Vera nor Rene told her of the spider, but wondered what it could have been.

Eddy's company was told that there was going to be a parade of Regular Army and Home Guard. First they had to go down to Tor Abbey lawns for a practise parade to see who was best. Mr Truman had his troop so well drilled that they led the parade.

Another day they had a shooting match on Walls Hill range against one of the Regular regiments from Denbury. Most of the old men in Eddy's platoon had been in the Great War. The seventy and eighty year olds had to wear their spectacles, but they were mustard with Lee Enfields. Again, the Home Guard emerged victorious.

In Eddy's platoon was an old man called George Browning. He was the lavatory cleaner down the town. He had a silver plate in his head, and his one ambition was to kill some more Germans. He lived behind the Palk Arms. His wife acted peculiarly whenever there was a full moon.

Eddy had to patrol with George. They had to make someone responsible for him. If George went with another Great War veteran – a little man called Osborne – they would go out to Walls Hill after drinking scrumpy in the back of the Masons Arms. After a few pints, they were liable to shoot anybody.

On Walls Hill the Home Guard had a lot of trouble with the Royal Air Force men from the hospital bringing their girls up there. There were Poles and Czechs as well as British pilots. The RAF were in the Palace and Cavendish Hotels. Eddy tripped over a couple on Walls Hill one night, and all he could see were the pilot's gleaming boots and the girl's white backside.

The Home Guard had to clear them off the cliff-top because when they lit up their fags their lighters were visible for miles. One night an RAF pilot answered George back. George pinned him against a tree with his bayonet – the point of the bayonet pressing against the pilot's lower lip. Even though he was old, George could throw a rifle with a bayonet on it like a dart.

Anstey's Cove formed a part of their patrol. They had to go round Walls Hill, down Anstey's Cove, and meet up in Ilsham Valley Road with the Marine Drive Home Guard. Eddy and George had met up with the Marine Drive Home Guard and were on their way back. A hut had been put up in the car park above Anstey's Cove. The bottom of the beach had been mined, and they had a machine gun post covering the path up from the beach. The night was wet and miserable. Eddy and George stood in the hut – soaked through. They had their rifles with them, fifty rounds each, and two hand grenades.

A little sports car came down, stopped in the car park.

"The bastard would stop here," George said.

"Ah, let him go," Eddy said.

"No. Rules is rules. Nobody allowed down here after sunset and before sunrise. You know that."

"Go on then," Eddy said.

So George stepped out of the hut, put his torch on, and approached the car. Eddy reluctantly followed him. Inside the car was a naval officer and his girl. The sports car had a celluloid flap on the door.

"Open the flap," George said. The officer had a chequered band around his cap.

"I beg your pardon?" he said. Eddy could see him thinking – a couple of Home Guard twats.

"You can't be deaf," George said, "or you wouldn't be an officer in His Majesty's Service. Open the flap."

The officer did not open the flap. George put up his rifle.

"You hear that one go up the spout?" he asked the officer.

"Steady on George," Eddy said.

The flap opened. "What do you want?"

"I'm asking you to move on, Sir," George said. "You're not allowed down here after sunset and before sunrise."

"Oh but you're only Home Guard," the officer said.

"So we may be ..." George said.

"We may be only Home Guard Sir," Eddy quickly said, "but we didn't come out here in dirty weather and make up all these rules ourselves. The rules are made by the Area Commander of the South West Area."

"Tut tut," the officer said.

"Open the door, Sir. Please," George said. "Bring the young lady, and start marching."

The officer was about to speak.

"If you refuse me," George said, "I'll blow your bloody head off."

"If I were you," Eddy told the officer, "I should do as he says."

So Eddy and George marched the officer and his girl through the rain up Walls Hill to what was a Boy Scout hut. Jack Perriman was on guard in the porch.

"Halt! Who goes there?"

"Anstey's Cove patrol returning with two prisoners," George sang out. Eddy heard Percy Bragg inside asking what the hell Browning had been up to this time.

Once inside the hut, all four of them dripping wet, the officer started to rant and to rave.

"Just a minute, Sir," Percy Bragg said. "I have to hear my patrol's report first." He asked George what had happened, then Eddy.

"It's quite simple," Eddy said. "We told him to move on, and he said: 'Home Guard? Who are you? Nothing.' So I told him we weren't out there all night for fun." And, quietly to Percy, Eddy added: "If we hadn't brought him along, George would've shot him."

"That's what I was afraid of," Percy said.

The officer was just starting to wax indignant again when in came Major Moore. He had once been an Admiral, was now in charge of all the Home Guard in Torquay. He had a peppery red face, always had a bottle of whisky with him.

"What's on then, Bragg?" he asked Percy.

"This chap ..." the officer began.

"You speak when you're spoken to First Lieutenant," Major Moore told him. "And I don't recall anyone telling you to stand at ease. You'll stand to attention until we speak to you."

Percy Bragg told Major Moore what had happened.

"So we're nothing, the Home Guard then? I suppose you can read? Being a First Lieutenant you would be able to read, wouldn't you?" And Major Moore proceeded to tick him off – in a dusty room, mattresses lying about the floor, in front of his girl, and in front of the Home Guard who had arrested him. He showed the officer the Home Guard rules and regulations – all signed by the Area General.

"I'm sorry," Major Moore said, "but I'm not having my chaps mucked about by the likes of you. Ring the police and have him put in for the night."

Percy appealed on the officer's behalf.

"Alright," Major Moore said. "Name, rank, number." The officer gave them to him. "Right," Major Moore told him. "You can now return with your young lady to your car, and you can go. But I'm afraid you won't be a First Lieutenant for long after this." And a week or so later Major Moore told them that the officer had been demoted.

Eddy's father was still working in the pottery in Newton Abbot. He refused to become a firewatcher.

"Bugger it," he said. "I fought six years in the Far East in the last war. If they wants fires watched, get the people down who owns it."

The Germans knocked hell out of Teignmouth. It had a small boat-building yard. They had no ack-ack anti-aircraft guns. One day a bloke told Eddy that he'd just seen two enemy planes playing a game with two horses – chasing the horses around a field – putting a burst of machine gun fire behind each horse to make it gallop.

One Sunday morning Eddy and George were walking in uniform along by the Palace on their way to drill.

"There's two officers coming," George said. "Just walk by and ignore 'em. Don't look right nor left."

"You're supposed to salute 'em," Eddy said.

"Do as I say," George said.

They walked past the two Regular officers.

"Excuse me," one of the officers called out to them. George and Eddy stopped.

"What are you two fellows?" the officer asked them.

"Home Guard," George said.

"You look like an old soldier," the officer said.

"I am an old soldier," George said. "I'm an Old Contemptible."

"Then you should have known better. You should have saluted us."

"Not you," George said. "I should have saluted the King's uniform."

"You should have saluted the King's uniform then. Why didn't you?"

"Because we're a guerrilla force."

"How do you make that out?"

"Well, when the invasion scare was here the other day, and we all stood to, and the OCO Western Command spoke to us, he told us that, in the event of the Germans landing, the Regulars would have to retreat and we'd have to fight in the hills and the caves. And, as we didn't come under the Regular Army, Jerry was quite within his rights to shoot all of us soon as he captured us. As guerrilla fighters, we don't come under the Geneva Convention. So, if I'm going to be shot, sod salutin' Regular officers."

The two officers were now laughing.

"Well to whom do you bear allegiance then?" they asked George.

"Captain Dampier," George said. "No other bugger."

"Do you drink?" they asked George.

"Oh yes, I like a drink."

"Well get you and your young mate one." And they gave him a ten bob note.

Morrison air-raid shelters were delivered to the house and the shop. They were like large tables, had thick iron legs and a steel top with wire netting around the sides. Providing the floor didn't collapse, the government claimed that the house could fall down about them and no-one would get hurt. Vera's customers went into her shelter down the shop.

One night a German plane, going on only one engine, limped back from Plymouth. It passed slowly over Walls Hill. Eddy could easily have shot the pilot, but they weren't allowed to shoot without permission, and by the time he ran back to the Boy Scout hut in the quarry to get permission the plane would have gone.

The Home Guard was issued with American rifles, hand grenades and Sten guns. They then divided the younger and the older men. The younger ones were made into a commando Home Guard and they went up to Haytor and Chudleigh to go through battle schools. They had to learn unarmed combat. Those with cars were given a petrol allowance; and if there was an invasion, it was their job to go out into the narrow country lanes, drop a tree in front of an enemy tank and lob Molotov cocktails on top of it.

There was to be a big exercise. The new commando Home Guard was to be the invaders against Regular troops in defence. The local papers told the people of the division. The Home Guard had to capture Dartmouth and Kingswear.

Knowing the country well, the Home Guard did not have much difficulty in getting to Kingswear. Eddy's platoon went into the Steam Packet for a drink. There were fifteen in his platoon.

"Pull us fifteen pints," Percy Bragg told the landlord. "Then the lot of you go down the cellar." The locals didn't believe him. He waved his Tommy gun at them. "I'm bloody serious. We're supposed to be Germans. And we want fifteen pints. Then you lot go down the cellar."

So the locals went down the cellar, were locked in, and each man in the platoon had his pint.

From there, they were going down one of Kingswear's steep streets when a woman threw a tin bath of cold water over Reg Hayman.

"You German buggers!" she called them. Reg Hayman never swore – the closest he came to swearing was to say flippin'.

"What d'you flippin' want to do that for missus?" he said, dripping wet.

"You'm a bloody German!" the woman shouted.

"Then I'll flippin' shoot you," Reg said.

They got to the pontoon where the ferry left Kingswear to cross to Dartmouth. Ken Ford and his two platoons of agricultural workers were already there. They had come from Dawlish, had been trained by a Royal Marine Sergeant. They were all of them hard. To get there they had hijacked a hearse – knocking out the undertakers to take it.

Meanwhile, across the river, the South Hams Home Guard had arrived on pony and, within an hour, had captured the whole of Dartmouth, the Royal Naval College, the Buffs Regiment and the artillery guns. The Regular troops had not expected the Home Guard to take the exercise so seriously.

The Regiment of Guards was stationed upriver at Galmpton. The Home Guard was informed by the umpires that the Guards were going to counter-attack in barges. Eddy's platoon and the others took up position around the pontoon. There were too many of them for comfort. Down came the Guards and tried to land. The ensuing battle became a little heated. One of the Guards hit one of the Dawlish Home Guard with the butt of his rifle.

"That's them then, boys!" the Dawlish Sergeant hollered. "If that's what they want, let's give it 'em!"

The Regiment of Guards was being thrown into the river when the umpires tried to call a halt. But the combatants were all so jammed in the narrow streets, punching and kicking and blanks going off, that no-one took any notice. Then over came three Hurricanes. Diving down they dropped bags of flour and soot.

To save the face of the Regular troops, the umpires said that owing to the Hurricanes coming to their relief the Regulars would have won. But in that case, the Home Guard said, the flour and soot landed over everyone so the Guards would have been knocked out as well. There was a stink over it afterwards – to think that a couple of Home Guard battalions could have so easily knocked out two Regular regiments.

Five

August 1940 – May 1941

August 1940: Germans continue bombing airfields.

August 24th 1940: First bombing of London.

August 25th 1940: First bombing of Berlin.

August 28th, 29th, 30th & 31st 1940: Merseyside bombed.

September 7th 1940: Mass incendiary bombing of London.

September 15th 1940: Decisive victory for RAF over London.

September 28th 1940: Hitler makes preparations for invasion of Russia. Blitz on London continues. Japan, Germany and Italy sign Tripartite Pact. Indo-China captured by Japanese against no resistance.

October 1940: Greeks repel Italian invasion. Burma road is re-opened for Chiang Kai'chek's supplies.

November 1940: Half the Italian fleet knocked out by British Fleet Air Arm at Taranto.

November 9th 1940: Chamberlain dies. Roosevelt re-elected.

November 14th 1940: Coventry bombed.

November 23rd, 30th & 31st: Southampton blitzed.

December 1940: General Wavell destroys Italian army in Suez. British bombing raid on Mannheim.

December 29th 1940: Second Fire of London.

January 3rd 1941: Bristol, Portsmouth, Cardiff and Manchester blitzed. Chunking still being bombed. Chiang Kai'chek and Mao Tse' Tung part. Thailand fighting Laos and Cambodia.

February 1941: Swansea and Glasgow blitzed. Rommel arrives in North Africa. Churchill's speech '... Give us the tools and we will finish the job ...'

March 1941: Rommel drives British back to Tobruk.

March 20th & 21st 1941: Plymouth blitzed – 18,000 houses destroyed.

April 1941: Germans invade Yugoslavia and Greece. Japanese-Soviet neutrality pact is signed.

April 21st, 22nd, 23rd, 28th & 29th 1941: Plymouth blitzed.

May 1941: Merseyside bombed for eight consecutive nights. Battle of Atlantic at peak.

May 10th 1941: Last night of London Blitz. Italians surrender Abyssinia. 'Bismarck' is sunk. 'Hood' is sunk. Germans occupy Crete.

May 31st 1941: First consignments of American aid arrive.

The morning after the first Plymouth blitz, six Devon General buses waited at Castle Circus for all the building men that Torquay could muster. They left at six, stopped to pick up more men in Paignton, and arrived in Plymouth at quarter to seven.

Eddy was dropped off in Chapel Street. All that Eddy could see was roads of broken glass. The first job was to get some blokes to shovel up the glass so that traffic could get into the city. Some of the Torquay masons were sent to repair roofs. Eddy was sent to help the Civil Defence in St Auburn Street. They were digging out a shelter.

In St Auburn Street were a market, pubs, Post Office and very old tenement houses. Eddy helped carry nine children out from the shelter. The oldest had been about ten, the youngest two. Blast force had killed them all – no obvious damage, just limp. The one Eddy carried was wearing Wellington boots. They took the bodies up to the next street, Chapel Street. Big tarpaulins were laid out on the grass behind the chapel. Eddy helped lay the bodies out, and then they pulled the tarpaulins over them.

The market in St Auburn Street had been bombed. The shelter had been under the market. The market had been full of potatoes. The potatoes had all been burnt. The Fire Brigade had managed to get most of the people out of the shelter. The potatoes had saved them. Eddy had never seen so many roast spuds in his life.

A policeman told Eddy and Harry Bunch to get a treble extension ladder to fetch a man down from a chimney. Blast had lifted a policeman two stories and had plastered him against the chimney stack. Eddy and Harry put ladders up on either side of the chimney. Then two men climbed up, held a bag between them, and scraped the remains out of the brickwork and into the bag.

The men who dug out were the experts. Eddy had to help wherever he was asked. He didn't get home until nine that night, sat in a chair and wept. He was excused Home Guard.

That night Eddy and Vera went to Vera's parents' to sleep. And that night the planes again came over on their way to Plymouth. They came roaring up over the copse and went on, large dark shapes droning overhead. Ned refused to come into the shelter, stood out on the path and cursed the planes.

"Bastards!" he shouted. "German bastards!" Then he called down into the shelter: "You alright?"

"Yes," Eddy said. "Come on down here and go to sleep."

Eddy was exhausted. And away in the distance they could see Plymouth burning like a big slow fire. Then on their way back, because British fighters were chasing them and they needed to lose weight for speed, the planes unloaded their remaining bombs onto Torquay.

While the blitz continued, Eddy went every day to Plymouth. He worked mostly in Devonport, in St Albans Terrace and Chapel Street, next to the dockyard. They were all tenement houses, once built for Drake's officers who fought the Spanish Armada centuries before, now slums. If the bombs hadn't killed people, was Eddy's opinion, the Luftwaffe would have performed a public service in clearing those slums.

The youngest and fittest bricklayers were sent to repair roofs – all of them four stories high and needing heavy treble extension ladders. They also had to knock down the plaster from the ceilings, replace it with white calico. They were allowed four pints of milk a day to wash down the black dust.

They went into one house where four prostitutes lived. Jim, the labourer, came running out, said that the fleas were marching up the walls.

A woman in the middle of St Albans Terrace had a parrot, a hen, cat and more birds. The houses on both sides of her got bombed, but she wouldn't leave unless they let her take her animals with her. Most of those who'd been bombed had been shifted out to the moors. She wouldn't go. One morning Eddy arrived to find her Anderson shelter almost blown over, with half the houses in the street nearly fallen down on top of it. She still refused to leave.

She was an extremely dirty woman. One of Eddy's labourers was called Freddy Strange. He was a lousy labourer, was a tailor by trade from Newton. His wife had loads of kids. He talked funny. He stared at this woman.

"What're you looking at?" she asked him.

"I'm looking at your titties," he said.

"Have a bloody good look," she said and pulled up her blouse. Two dirty breasts flopped out. Eddy and Jim Tozer didn't know what to do. Jim Tozer had been a marine in the Great War. He was very clean.

"Bloody hell," he said. "I've seen tits all over the world. Those two could do with a bloody good scrub."

"Don't be so bloody saucy," she said.

Freddy was a randy little bugger. They'd had to chuck him out of hospital for trying to get into bed with his wife two days after she'd had a baby.

"I'm gonna wop my Minnie," he'd said. And later on Freddy crept back to wop the parrot woman with the dirty breasts. In the end they forced her out, together with the thousands of others who went nightly up the moors.

Every night huge bonfires were lit on the unoccupied parts of the moors in the hope that the Germans would be misled into dropping their bombs there. Some did. Most didn't.

The mornings after the bombings, signs would appear on heaps of rubble saying: 'Up the Nazis', 'Heil Hitler'. Some were in German, some in English.

In St Barnaby Park Eddy completely re-roofed two houses, slates and all. Next morning all five houses were gone. A bomb disposal squad was blown up in St Barnaby Park. They were blown clean over the houses and into the next road.

One day Eddy was working on the roof of Aggie Weston's, a rest home for sailors. Most of the houses around it were down. Those that hadn't been wholly bombed had been dynamited. Aggie Weston's had been roped off. Engineers and police waited below while Eddy and Freddy went up the fire escape and onto a flat roof above the damage. Eddy was tied on with a bosun's hitch and let down to a sloping roof where there were forty or fifty slates missing in one big hole. Eddy and Freddy began tapping away to fill it. A Royal Engineer waved to them from below.

Eddy told Freddy to stop tapping. "That bloke's going bloody frantic down there," he explained.

"Looks like the bugger wants us to come down," Freddy said.

"Pull up quick!" Eddy shouted to the men on the flat roof. "Bugger the tools," he told Freddy, and they ran down the fire escape. No sooner had they got to the bottom than the whole building – all nine stories of it – collapsed in on itself. The dynamiting and bombing had weakened the foundations. Eddy got a new set of tools out of it.

Some women caught two German pilots who had bailed out over Devonport. That was the last seen of them.

Eddy was sent to repair a hole in one of the roofs of Sunshine Terrace. They were better class houses that overlooked the Sound, had once housed Lord Nelson's Admirals. The roofs had small parapets. The hole in the roof was oblong. Eddy looked in through the hole. Resting on the roof joists was a paving slab. The ceiling below wasn't damaged. The labourers searched the three surrounding streets but couldn't find where the paving stone could have come from.

In the cellar of the same house they found a man's leg. They reported it to the police – as they did all the bodily bits and pieces they found. The police came up and put a sack over it, and later someone came round with tin dustbins picking up all the limbs on their list and taking them to the incinerator. When a site had been badly bombed, and there were known to be a lot of dead in it, then it was all bulldozed in and covered with chlorate of lime.

All in all, Plymouth was a balls-up. The Fire Brigades from outside Plymouth arrived with the wrong fittings on their hosepipes, so even if there had been any water, they wouldn't have been able to do anything. So another job Eddy was given was to keep damping down fires with buckets of water until the Fire Brigade arrived.

A house between Chapel Street and Hilary Street was still smoking. Harry Bunch went up a ladder and they passed buckets of water up to him to throw into the room. The fire stopped smouldering.

"I'll go in and have a look round," Harry said.

"Don't know if there's any floor joists," Eddy said. "Test a bit."

Harry went in first. He called to Eddy: "You'd better come up here, see what you think. It looks like a tailor's dummy here in the corner – burnt. Everything's charred up here."

Eddy went up and had a look. "It's a bloke, I think," he said. "You can see where his cock's been." There was a charred lump there.

"Getaway," Harry said. Eddy picked up a bit of lath that had fallen from the ceiling, poked it into the tailor's dummy. The lath went right through.

Between the wall and the dummy they found a gas mask case and a naval steel helmet. They reported it to the police, and the police said they would put a number on it and someone would collect what was left of it.

When the police had gone, a woman with three children came over to Eddy and Harry.

"Have you seen anyone in there?" she asked them.

"No. Nobody in there," Eddy said. "Why?"

"That was our flat. And we all went across to the shelter. But my husband left some money – his savings – and he went back to get it."

Then Eddy could see what had happened. The man had gone back, a rafter had come down and knocked him out, and the poor sod had been burnt to death. And why they'd thought it a tailor's dummy was because only the torso remained – the arms and legs had been burned off.

Cyril Perry came home on leave. Rene gave a party. They all tried to talk cheerfully, to ignore the planes going overhead on their way to Plymouth. Eddy hadn't yet arrived back from Plymouth, was going to come to the party later. Suddenly the siren went. They all immediately jammed into the cupboard under Rene and Cyril's stairs.

Eddy had meanwhile come home, was standing with Ned on the lawn in Congella Road watching the planes go over. A bomb went up on top of the copse – a bloody great flash. And in the first house in Princess Road West, at the bottom of Rene's road, a light was shining like a beacon through somebody's door.

"I'm going down to see about that light," Eddy told Ned. "Then I'll go up and see how the party's going."

When he got down to the house with the light, there were two or three people standing around the door. The door had glass in it.

"Anybody in that house?" Eddy asked a man.

"No. And we can't get in," the man said. "The bloody door's locked."

"They could beam down on that light," Eddy said. So he picked up a stone out of the rockery, heaved it through the glass and switched the light off.

When Eddy got down to Rene and Cyril's he went into the kitchen. The house looked empty. He turned a whistling kettle off on the stove. Then all the others emerged sheepishly from under the stairs. Rene had forgotten she'd put the kettle on, and they'd mistaken its whistle for the siren.

The owner of the house whose glass door Eddy had smashed came up to Congella Road to claim damages off Eddy.

"What're you going to do about it?" Eddy asked him. "You can summons me if you like. You were bloody daft leaving that light on." Eddy heard no more from him.

The bomb that he and Ned had seen go off above the copse had landed on the house of the Chief Air Raid Warden of Torquay, killing the man and all his family.

In Plymouth, the naval dockyards had taken heavy bombing. Eddy saw them bringing the corpses out of there in red Devon

General buses with their windows painted black. And while Eddy and others like him moved in to clear up the wreckage, others were busy looting. All the suits were looted out of Burtons.

"Bloody marvellous," a policeman said to Eddy. "There's us got to come out and risk our lives, and there's them buggers risking their lives looting."

After a while the police tightened up on the looting. Eddy and the rest were searched on their way home. Those that were caught said: "What of it? There's no bugger here."

"How would you like it if everything was taken out of your bloody house?" the police responded.

The only thing that Eddy took home was four goldfish and a tortoise.

He was repairing a roof in St Hilary Terrace. In the back garden of the house was a pond. It was full of slates. He heard the tortoise crying, and rescued that. Then he saw something flash from the sun in the pond. He pulled back the slates and found the goldfish. They all had cuts on their sides where the slates had nicked them. Eddy put them in an old bucket, kept changing the water until half past six when he went home. Horace, Harry, Henry and Hedward, Vera called them. Hedward was the biggest. They put them in their pond in Congella – an old cast iron bath sunk into the ground. Later the fish learned to eat bread out of Ned's hand. Fred Monk had the tortoise.

The women in Plymouth cooked in biscuit tins over open fires. Eddy one day fixed a roof for an old woman. He had to be lowered upside down on a rope to fix the last slates. When he came down from the roof the old woman had cooked them a complete roast dinner in one biscuit tin.

Blast did funny things. A labourer from Chelston, about fifty-years-old, put a ladder up against a chimney. But blast had sliced through the chimney and the chimney had pitched back exactly in place. When the labourer put the ladder up against the chimney the whole stack toppled over, landed on top of him and killed him.

Blast did funny things. Eddy found four people in a cellar sitting around a table – two men and two women – their meal before them. He touched one of them, and all four fell over. The blast had the effect of drowning in air – filling the lungs with air and then immediately sucking it all out.

Night time, the people went frantic to get away before the blitz started. The men who were working there too.

"Bloody shame," the foreman said, "to have some of these bastards working here."

In St Hilary Terrace every ceiling was down. In each street they picked one house as a store. Slates and nails were kept there so that if the repair gangs wanted anything they wouldn't have far to go. Upstairs was furniture, locked up. One day a woman came from the store house in St Hilary Terrace. She was playing up hell – there was no furniture left. She accused everyone of taking it.

"Well a furniture van came and took that," a bloke said. "It had Brown and something on it. Brown and Co.. Said they had to take it out to Launceston." There turned out to be gangs going round, watching to see where the furniture was being stored, stealing it all and then selling it.

Vera's rations for a week were now a tiny piece of butter, a tiny piece of cheese, one egg each, a quarter pound of tea, and some dehydrated potato, which was like eating soap. They were allowed two ounces of meat each, sometimes liver, but no bacon. There were plenty of vegetables though, so they lived mostly on stews.

Freddy could get anything. He had the knack. So, instead of helping the others, he was out in Plymouth all day shopping.

"Freddy, see if you can get us some biscuits," Eddy would say. Others would ask for other things; and so Freddy would be gone all day trying to buy all that he could.

There was a bit of a fiddle going on among the builders in Plymouth, money changing hands, the masons being sent to repair houses of people who had status. One dinner time Eddy was doing an old lady's roof. Cavannagh the builder came up and told him that he had to go to another terrace and work on a big house there.

"There's only three slates off it," Eddy said. "I'm staying here till I've finished this old lady's roof. She's seventy odd. Poor old sod."

"Don't forget you're army age," Cavannagh said. "Could be reported."

"You fuckin' well report me then," Eddy said.

When they finished the old lady's house they did go up to the big house. Freddy tagged along with Eddy and Jim. Freddy was handy for piddling about, fetching a nail or a slate. The owner of the big house was a decent enough chap, made them all a cup of tea. He was wearing a beautiful suit. Eddy and Jim went up and fixed his three slates. The man was very pleased, gave them a couple of shillings each.

"Excuse me, Sir," Freddy said. "That's a lovely suit. But the waistcoat spoils it. Waistcoat's all wrong. Don't fit at all." The man didn't know what to say.

"Does he know anything about tailoring?" he asked Eddy.

"He's a first class tailor," Eddy said. "If he says the waistcoat's wrong, it is."

" 'Twon't take me half'n hour to do it for you, Sir," Freddy said.

Freddy always carried his tailoring stuff in a big wallet. Out it came. He took the man's jacket off, put a chalk mark here, a pin there. The man was so pleased with the result that he gave Freddy two pounds. Two pound fifteen was a week's wages.

"That bastard isn't so bloody silly," Jim Tozer said.

Ten to six in the morning the coaches left Castle Circus. Three quarters of an hour later they were in Plymouth. The coach drivers raced to be first there, had a competition between themselves. The men said they never seemed to get home so quick at night. Then they left at six-thirty, got home at nine.

Every night, Eddy came home covered in fleas and had a bath. Then he ate his supper without a word, not telling Vera of what he had seen during the day. And then he went to bed. But he didn't sleep. Each night, on the path outside, Ned would be pacing up and down.

"They're coming over, boy!" he'd shout. And Eddy would hear the drone, see the searchlights, and listen to Ned going up and down.

"They're coming over!"

Come the end, Eddy was so fed up with him that he stuffed all the bedding into the shelter and slept there.

Six

June 1941 – November 1941

June 1941: Hull is blitzed.

June 22nd 1941 4am: Germany attacks Russia.

July 3rd 1941: Stalin announces 'scorched earth' policy. Hull blitzed again. Japanese troops occupy whole of Indo-China.

August 12th 1941: Churchill and Roosevelt sign 'Atlantic Charter'. Butt Report states that strategic bombing is ineffective, recommends area bombing.

September 22nd 1941: 'Tanks for Russia' week. Mermansk convoys begin.

October 1941: New Japanese government formed under General Hideki Tojo. Lord Croft's Pikes, which were bayonets welded onto the end of a piece of copper pipe, issued to Home Guard.

November 1941: Auchinleck occupies Cyrenacia. Food rationing becomes tighter. Seventh raid on Berlin (169 out of 400 bombers fail to return).

Eddy was sent back to Holywell to work on an isolated hotel. It overlooked a large beach and sand dunes. Four bankrupt men were in charge of the job. Eddy could earn good money if he put in long hours. The men working on the site came from Cornwall, London and Ireland. They were allowed into Newquay once a week.

When they had finished one part of the hotel the first lot of troops arrived. The soldiers had to run up and down the dunes, which disturbed the sand. The fine sand blew in and covered all the fields, made it look like desert. The brickies wondered when the Nile would flood. Once a month Eddy came home by coach.

Mr and Mrs Endicott, the betting-shop bookies, lived opposite the Country House pub. The authorities filled their small house with evacuees. One woman staying there had three children. She sent one of the girls over to Maison Vee's to have her hair cut.

Vera sat the girl in the chair, started to comb her hair through. The hair was alive with lice. Vera had never seen lice so big and so many on one head. Trying not to let the girl see what she was doing, Vera immediately burnt everything that the girl had come into contact with – the towel, the comb, her own gown – so that the lice wouldn't get passed on to any of her other customers.

She sent the girl back to the Endicotts with a note for her mother. Vera had tried to be as diplomatic as possible, '... afraid I was unable to cut your daughter's hair. Are you aware that your daughter has lice?'

The mother came barging into the shop. She was a Cockney.

"You bastard!" she screamed at Vera. "You smug bugger. My children been livin' in the shelters three months ..."

Vera felt mean, and sorry for them, but she couldn't let her other customers catch lice.

After that, she checked all evacuees' hair for lice. They all had them. Mrs Endicott caught lice off them – they all had to live in the same room. And Mrs Endicott normally had her hair done every week – it was very long, her crowning glory. And with hair that long she had a hell of a job getting rid of them. So keeping aside scissors, comb and gown for Mrs Endicott, Vera did her hair at home every evening, washing it with Derbox soap. Within a week she had cleared them.

Eddy was told he would be going next to a factory in Stoke-on-Trent, which suited him. Even though at night the Germans bombed it. Some of his friends had gone there with a Cockney. The factory being so huge, they had trams inside it to take them from place to place. The Cockney had told one of the bricklayers to get on the tram and go up to another section and book in on the night shift there. So they booked in, got their tickets and then sneaked off home to their digs. Then they got up early in the morning, went in and booked off the night shift, and then signed on for their own shift. They had all been on double wages.

But come the end, Eddy wasn't sent to Stoke-on-Trent. He was sent to Corsham instead. The work in Corsham was underground. He had to brick up old chalk pits for an ammunition store. The natural caverns went on for miles, complete with railway tracks and lighting. From there, he was sent back to Padstow, to Treginnon aerodrome.

Inside Maison Vee's they couldn't hear the sirens for the sound of the hairdryers. So, as soon as a raid started, the air-raid wardens telephoned Maison Vee's. Quite often, it was too late.

One day Vera had Mrs Wyatt, the chemist's wife, in for a permanent wave. That meant that Mrs Wyatt's hair had to be wired up to the ceiling by about fifty separate wires; and each individual curler had to be worked off because the paper stuck to the rollers. Suddenly the bombs started to drop. The planes were coming over right down the valley. Vera put her arms around all the wires, wrenched them from the ceiling and bundled Mrs Wyatt out the back of the shop and into the shelter.

Afterwards Vera said: "Mrs Wyatt, I'm ever so sorry."

"God almighty, my dear," Mrs Wyatt said. "Thank God you did it. How you ever stopped and took them off I'll never know."

Mrs Wyatt was a diabetic and her hair never took the perm properly. Vera kept brandy for the air raids: when this one was over she passed it around the girls and the customers to soothe their nerves. Then she realised that she had no idea how long Mrs Wyatt's hair had been steamed. The curlers had cooled. So she started again, did it by guesswork; and Mrs Wyatt ended up with the best perm she ever had.

During that same raid Bere's hairdressers in Tor Hill Road was hit; an Auxiliary Territorial Service girl, who had run out of the Regal, was cut in half by machine gun fire.

From Padstow, Eddy was sent to Puriton where an ammunition factory was being built in a marsh. It had to be in a marsh because of the amount of water needed to make the ammunition. Sabu was powerful stuff.

All the labourers on the site were women from London. They wore turbans. The first morning Eddy was there, it was frosty. Lew Craddick bent over to pick up some blocks. A woman labourer came up behind him, grabbed hold of his goolies.

"Blimey, they're tight this morning mate," she said.

Though they were not allowed to smoke, the women always had a cigarette on them. When they wanted a smoke, they stood next to a steam jet.

One day, two German planes crashed nearby. About three hundred people, armed with pudlocks – transverse scaffolding poles – and lump hammers, chased the airmen who had parachuted out of them. The London women were particularly mad; they had been bombed out of Covent Garden. The Germans were terrified. Luckily for them, the security police got to them first.

The site was overrun with rats, brown and black. They had to be killed in case they undermined the foundations. So the Friday of every week was ratting day. Nobody worked. Some men would go along and squirt gas into every hole in the bank. The rest stood by with pickaxes, shovels and pudlocks to kill any rats that ran out.

Eddy came home for the August bank holiday. The train from Puriton was packed. In the Daily Mirror and in all the other papers it said that the British people were ignoring the war and that they were all going to Torquay, Paignton and Cornwall for the weekend.

"This bloody stupid propaganda," Eddy said. "We're going to get bombed. Jerry's going to start strafing everywhere."

Vera had been saving eggs for when Eddy got home. Dinner had just been dished up when, at one o'clock exactly – Eddy looked at the clock – he heard the planes.

"That's Focke-Wolfes," he said.

"What?" Ned said.

"Them's bloody Germans!" Eddy said. Vera just had time to see a plane filling the window before Eddy pushed her and her mother into the cupboard under the stairs. Ned refused to go. He got nasty. Eddy booted him up the backside, shut the cupboard door on him and then lay down in the passageway.

He saw a plane come down the valley skimming the roofs, saw the bomb come out. The ack-ack they had in Torquay wasn't up to much. They had two guns out on Walls Hill, but the planes came in so low that they couldn't get the trajectory down far enough to fire at them. Eddy heard the bomb go off. *Oh Christ,* he thought, *Alexander Road. Vera's shop.*

The bomb hit four houses in Alexander Road and killed some people. In Maison Vee's the ceiling was down, all the basins were broken and there was glass everywhere. Eddy put on his Home Guard denims to clear up the mess. Neighbours came to help.

Vera kept a float of ten one-shilling pieces in small change in her till. The till had been blown across the shop. Yet, from amongst the debris, they managed to find all ten shillings.

And, although in that raid the planes had strafed the whole of the seafront, no-one had been hit. The army had taken over the Palm Court Hotel, and outside they had an old Lewis gun from the first war. The army cook had used it to shoot one plane down. The army also had a Bofors out on the end of Princess Pier. Harry had been in charge of that. But instead of shooting down any planes, he had shot a hole through the Pavillion. He got court martialled for that.

It took months to get the shop repaired, although the basins were fixed next day so that Vera could boast 'Business As Usual'. But the windows stayed boarded up and the ceilings were never fixed.

At Puriton, money seemed no object. They wanted to put a mound over one magazine. But next to it was a load of scaffolding. It had been there a long time.

Charles Bran, the boss, said: "Bury it." So they put a mound over two thousand pounds worth of scaffold.

For every man Charles Bran hired he got twenty percent of his wages, and for all materials eighteen percent of their cost. And no man could leave. They even got fined if they were late for work or caught skiving. And they had to work Saturdays whether there was anything to do or not.

Eddy got extra for his job. Huge pits were dug out, and then concrete walls three-feet thick were put up, with little outlets for pipes. Eddy then had to line the floor with white brick, and the sides with brown brick. For cement they used a mixture called

Corax, which was like soluble rubber. The labourers mixed a black powder with it. Within an hour, the four-inch wall could be hit with a sledgehammer and it wouldn't budge. Eddy was paid extra because the acid that they made the explosive from was so strong and dangerous. The concrete pit would only last two years, then have to be ripped out and replaced.

Across each pit was a safety bridge. One day one of the women going across the bridge fell off into the acid. One of the brickies saw her fall, said that within six minutes there was only a skeleton left.

Everyone on the site had a mask issued to them. When the wind blew the yellow smoke from the chimneys towards them, it felt as if pins and needles were sticking into their faces. And if they scratched their skin, they dug themselves raw. The men who worked inside the magazines got a fabulous wage. But they all looked like Chinamen.

After Puriton, Eddy worked at Barton Hall in Torquay – converting it into a training place for fire brigades. While he was there, he had to perform Home Guard duty on two nights each week.

One Sunday he and Vera were returning from fishing down at Long Quarry. They were half way up the cliff path. "My Christ!" Eddy said. "Here they come!" Four planes were coming towards them just above the water. Eddy pressed Vera into the path. As the planes reached the cliff, they zoomed up. The sirens had not sounded. The planes were too low for the radar. One went up over Vera and Eddy, and the other three went up over Babbacombe cliff.

Eddy was sent to Tiverton, then Dunkeswell. At Dunkeswell, he had to build the hospital department on the airfield. They had many tip-and-run raids there. Dummy aircraft had been laid out across the airfield. The Germans shot these up.

91

Most of Eddy's work was putting up brick partitions inside Nissen huts for hospital wards. One day a German plane fired its machine guns along the length of a Nissen hut in which Eddy was working. The noise was terrifying, but he wasn't hit.

He had lodgings in Exeter. His landlady fed him well. One weekend Vera went up to stay with him. But Eddy still had to work the Saturday and Sunday so she hardly saw him. And that weekend Exeter had its worst raid yet.

Seven

November 21st 1941 – January 1942

December 2nd 1941: Conscription of women announced. Germans reach outskirts of Moscow.

December 7th 1941: Pearl Harbour bombed by the Japanese. USA and Britain declare war on Japan. Thailand agrees to Japanese occupation.

December 8th 1941: Malaya invaded.

December 11th 1941: Germany and Italy declare war on USA.

December 13th 1941: British forces withdrawn from Thailand.

December 21st 1941: Japanese occupy Victoria Point, South Burma.

December 23rd 1941: Japanese bomb Rangoon.

December 25th 1941: British surrender Hong Kong to the Japanese.

January 1942: Rommel recaptures Benghazi. MacArthur defends Philippines against the Japanese.

January 4th 1942: Kuontam taken by the Japanese.

January 7th 1942: Kuala Lumpur abandoned by British troops.

January 10th 1942: 'Prince of Wales' and 'Repulse' sunk by Japanese.

January 11th 1942: Kuala Lumpur taken by Japanese.

January 20th 1942: Japanese invade Burma.

January 26th 1942: First batch of GIs arrive in Britain.

Most of the building work on the aerodromes was finished. There were scores of men who were not of army age to do the repair jobs. Many of them were in London clearing up after The Blitz. Now every man who was of army age had to go for a medical.

Eddy was told on the Thursday that he would have to go for his medical, and he was given a free train pass. He went home on the Saturday and returned to Exeter on Sunday with a crowd of others from Torquay.

The medicals were being held in the Castle Chambers. They all went for a drink before reporting there. The first thing they had to do for the medical was pee in a bottle. Baron Hingston was a big man, always drunk, never bothered with digs, slept out rough – in air-raid shelters, anywhere.

He said to the doctor: "Haven't you got a few buckets? I can't stop pissing just because you've only given me this bottle."

"You shouldn't be having medicals at all," the doctor said. "You've all been drinking."

They had cubicles curtained off for each test. Eddy reached the heart cubicle. They strapped gadgets to him, made him jump up and down, up and down, until he was near worn out. Tom Hicks the bricklayer had a bad heart but hadn't known about it until the medical. Although he had never been ill in his life before then, Tom Hicks was given an envelope and told to go straight home to his doctor. He hadn't worked since. The army doctors had been unable to figure out how he had lived up until then, his heart was so bad. And Tom was a big raw-boned man. And Harold Bradcock discovered that he had a defective knee. And he had been all right up until then too.

Eddy was sent on to the next cubicle. They had taken so long he suspected that he, too, had something wrong with him. But he passed all their tests, including the one where they held his testicles and he coughed.

In front of Eddy was a farmboy from Sidmouth. He was so big that Eddy couldn't see either side of him.

"I never ought to be here you know," he told Eddy. "My lungs is in a terrible state. Can't breathe. And I've got flat feet." This list of ailments was repeated continually as they waited.

They reached the last doctor. He was an old man of seventy-eight. Eddy sized him up, decided that he was a cute old bugger. The farmboy started moaning as soon as he got to him.

"I don't know doctor, it's a mistake my being here. I've got bad lungs, can hardly breathe."

"Oh yes," the old doctor said. "And you can't stand up?"

"No. I've got these flat feet."

"Oh dear," the doctor said. "You are in a state. Get your trousers down, both of you." Eddy and the farmboy dropped their trousers. "Come outside the cubicle."

Eddy saw the doctor walk around behind them. He had a funny little pocket up the vent of his coat. He pulled out a hammer.

"You did say you were having trouble with your feet?" he said chattily to the farmboy as he picked up his foot. He banged it with the hammer. The farmboy yelled and leapt in the air.

"Ah my son," the doctor said. "I'm seventy-eight. Too old for you. I only wish I was as fit as you." The farmboy left protesting.

The doctor tapped Eddy with the hammer, but not so hard.

"You're A-One," he said.

"Well I've been worried," Eddy said, "about this heart business."

"Oh yes. Of course. That's because your heart is two inches out of ocean centre."

"What's that mean?" Eddy said.

"Your heart is over this way two inches more than it should be. It isn't common, but it does happen. It doesn't affect the workings of your heart. Really, you've not changed much since prehistoric times. Prehistoric men had their heart in the centre."

Baron Hingston also passed A1.

Eddy went back to the job and told them he was A1. He was paid up, had a fortnight at home before he had to go to Colchester.

Vera had not expected Eddy to pass, seeing how he was always moaning about his health. Just the luck of the draw, Eddy said.

Herb had also passed, had joined the Navy and was on a small aircraft carrier.

Cyril Perry was in the Redcaps looking after prisoners.

Cyril Drew was in the Civil Defence.

Cyril Blackler was in the Royal Engineers.

Bert Ewens was in the army dance band.

Frank Soper was guarding the gasworks.

Mac had been sent to Gibraltar.

Bill Gill had been sent up to Lincolnshire in the RAF.

Les Ellis, Eileen's husband, had joined the Field Engineers, had been sent out to the desert. One day Les was itching like hell. He went to the Medical Officer. The MO told him that he had the crabs, that he would have to walk back to the depot and get himself a complete new uniform. The depot was four miles away.

Les walked across the desert. At the depot they took his uniform away, shaved his genitals and plastered them with blue unction and painted it everywhere else there was hair – on his chest, under his arms. It was a purple blue. They burned his uniform, said that they would send another up the line to him.

So, wearing only his boots, and carrying his rifle, Les started off on the four miles back to the line. He wasn't particularly worried about having no clothes on, as they hadn't seen anyone for months. So, with his purple-blue chest and other parts, he plodded on across the desert. Out of the blue came a convoy of Auxilliary Territorial Service girls.

As each lorry passed him the girls called out: "Pretty Poll! Pretty Poll!"

On December 5th 1941, Eddy, George Downer and another man caught the train to Colchester to begin army training. Eddy had to wear his Home Guard uniform. It was snowing when they arrived. They were told to parade. The Non-Commissioned Officers told Eddy and the others in Home Guard uniform that they knew bugger all.

Eddy said nothing.

Peter Wilson, the radio commentator, was the Liaison Officer. He noted down all the recruits' personal details. Because Eddy had been to Newton Abbot Secondary School, and because it had run its own Boy Cadets, Eddy was marked down as a potential NCO. If he had been to grammar school he would have been labelled as potential officer material.

The Physical Education Instructors all had high squeaky voices. The six assistant spring-heeled Jacks all copied the chief spring-heeled Jack.

Their second day there, all the recruits lined up stripped in the gym. Spring-heeled Jack looked them over.

"How old would you be then? Stand up straight when I'm talking to you!"

"Twenty-eight, Sergeant Major."

"You sure?" And to the Sergeant behind him: "Do you think so Sergeant? Do you think it's possible that this man is twenty-eight years old? I'd say fifty-one at least. What do you say?"

After insulting almost everyone like this, he asked what they had been doing to get themselves into such a state; and he told them how they would ache, how their muscles would complain, but how at the end of their eight weeks they would be either fit enough to jump over the gym, or be physical wrecks. The conscripts all considered him to be a seriously hard bastard.

The first weekend in Colchester they all lined up for an injection. Shirts off, they queued outside the hut. It was freezing.

"Right arm up!" They shuffled along. Their only hope was that the doctor changed the needle just before they reached the hut, else it was going to be blunt. Some men fainted – big men as well. Afterwards they were confined to camp for a week because of possible side effects. Eddy felt sick and feverish for a couple of days but otherwise he was all right.

The following Saturday, they queued outside the hut again. Again with their shirts off.

"Right arm up!" they were ordered. That puzzled Eddy; he had been told the next injection would be in the other arm. He thought he ought to say something in case this was a mistake. They injected about two dozen by the time they reached Eddy. He hadn't bothered saying anything to the Sergeant, would only have had his head shouted off.

The doctor was Canadian.

"Excuse me, Sir," Eddy said to him. "Is this the first injection?"

"Why?" the doctor snapped.

"We had this done last Saturday, Sir," Eddy said. "We've been in two weeks now."

"Christ!" the doctor shouted. "Stop everything!" There was a panic. The Sergeant came running up.

"You bloody fool Sergeant!" the doctor screamed at him. The Sergeant went pale. Those who had been injected the second time were rushed to hospital. Eddy and the rest were dismissed until the next weekend, when they were given the other injection in the left arm.

They were allowed to go down into Colchester. The conscripts wore Bakelite badges, so everyone knew they were rookies. One day they saw Spring-heeled Jack pushing a pram, with his wife and five children walking in front, and his wife was giving him a tongue-lashing. After that, they did not take him so seriously. Eddy told one of the other Sergeants about it back at the gym.

"So you found out then," this Sergeant said. "That's why he's such a bastard up here."

A few weeks into his army service Eddy read in the papers that Torquay had suffered another tip-and-run raid. The Germans had dropped bouncing bombs on Ellacombe and many roofs had been damaged, ceilings brought down. Eddy wrote to ask Vera if the roof of their house had been damaged, hoping that she would say that it had, and he could get a week's leave. But Vera didn't want Eddy to worry, so she wrote back telling him everything was fine. Eddy did not get his leave.

Vera and Rene had nicknames for their customers. There was Mrs Bristletine, Mrs Her-Were-With-Me, Mrs Wind In The Willows – because when she was under the drier, and thinking nobody could hear for the noise of the drier, she would fart. There was Aunt Fanny, Minnie Ha-Ha, Mrs Thtevens.

Then there was Ol' Smelly Belly, who had ulcers on her legs and liked the men; and who also had an Alsatian dog with a large undercarriage – the girls in the shop reckoned she used to do it with the dog when she couldn't get a man. There was Missus V – because that was all she would call Vera. And Tosser-Offer-Dora, Old Cockles and Old Wibby Webber.

Every conscript in Colchester, no matter if he was going to be a cook, a clerk or a lorry driver, had to be trained for combat, whereas before the war if someone had joined the army as a lorry driver then that was all they did. The British Army had learned some harsh lessons.

When they brought the Sten guns out on the range, Eddy decided to keep to himself the fact he had already handled them in the Home Guard. A truck driver was the first to try out the Sten. He didn't hold it tight enough, the Sten gun jumped about, and everyone dived for the ground, bullets whizzing everywhere.

They had to aim at petrol tins, keep the tin moving with the force of the bullets. Eddy took the gun, kept the tin moving along the ground.

"You used a Sten before?" the officer asked him.

"No Sir," Eddy lied.

"You're bloody good," the officer said.

The Sergeant was from Brixham. "Come on," he said to Eddy. "You had these buggers in the Home Guard. I just tumbled to that."

Vera, Rene, and the rest of the shop were conscripted into the ARP. They were each given a white tin hat, with ARP painted on it, and a whistle. They were given their training in a hut behind the Palk Arms.

Neither Vera nor Rene took in any of their training. They blamed the tin hats. Soon as they put them on, they started giggling. Rene's hat was too small, wobbled about on top of her head. And Vera's hat was too big, rested on her glasses. When Vera turned her head the hat stayed still. Then, when the instructor came to show them how to work a fire extinguisher – a stirrup pump – Rene pressed hers by accident and sprayed the instructor.

When they were called out in a raid, Vera would be in her street, with her hat and her whistle, thinking, *Here I am on my own in my street and up there, in her street, on her own, is my friend*

Rene, with her hat and her whistle. And she wondered, whatever would they do if anything happened?

Eddy was put into the Dorsets. The Sergeant Major told everyone over five feet ten inches tall to 'One Step Forward March'.

"You lot are going for a special medical."

They were given a four-day examination. Eyes, ears, inside, outside, feet ... No-one told them what it was for, and it was pointless asking.

The last doctor to see them was another Canadian. He looked at their feet. The Sergeant Major was out of the way so Eddy asked the doctor what the medical was for.

"Don't you know, boy?" The Canadians didn't speak posh like British doctors. "Between you and me, if you pass this then you're A1 plus, and you can be put into the paratroops or the airborne. In your case you can't go into the paratroops – you've got five or six false teeth. But you can go into the airborne, or the pack artillery, the commando artillery, or the commandos. Or in any of the other special regiments. If you can avoid it, don't go into the pack artillery – that kills more than any other. Not the action – you just get buggered up pushing mules over mountains. There's more graded down have been in that than have been in the commandos."

"Thanks very much," Eddy said. He got A1 plus and was sent to Harrogate in Yorkshire.

Eight

February – March 1942

February 1942: Home Guard becomes compulsory service.

February 14th 1942: Directive to Bomber Command states, '... focus on morale of civilian population'.

February 15th 1942: General Percival surrenders Singapore to Japan. 90,000 troops taken prisoner.

February 23rd 1942: 'Bomber' Harris becomes Commander of Chief Bomber Command.

February 25th 1942: Petrol and clothes rationing begins.

March 8th 1942: Dutch East Indies surrenders to Japan. Rangoon is occupied.

March 28th & 29th 1942: Lubeck is destroyed by British bombers.

Eddy was sent to a Hore Belisha camp on the moors about fifteen miles from Harrogate. There they had an infantry commando course and a gun commando course. Eddy was to learn how to handle twenty-five-pounders. But they didn't have any self-propelled twenty-five-pounders, so he had to learn on ordinary guns. And they didn't have enough guns, so they had to exercise out on the Yorkshire moors as infantry one week, then on the guns for the next. When they were training as commandos they had to sleep in swamps for three nights, then pretend to be infantry while those on the guns fired over them.

Eddy was put in a barracks with thirty-two Irishmen. Eddy and a little Jewish boy were the only English in there. The Jewish boy had been put there by mistake. His feet turned out; and his father made shirts in a fashionable shop in Piccadilly – handmade shirts.

"Bloody Commando Artillery!" the Sergeant said. "How'd you get sent here?"

"I don't know," he said. Jews were usually made company tailor. The Irish blokes scrounged money off him. He was too afraid to refuse.

Every Sunday in the barrack was murder. Some of the Irish were Orange Men, some Sinn Fein. They boozed Sunday lunchtime and the afternoon was full of arguments. Although the country boys were not so bad.

Burkee was the leader of the Irish – big and powerful, and thick. His forehead wasn't much more than a half-inch high. He had kicked someone's eye out.

A timber merchant's son from Hull was made unpaid lance-jack in charge of the barrack. The poor little sod couldn't even salute properly. And the Irish were good soldiers – shit hot at drill, couldn't be faulted.

One morning all the Irish came in at four o'clock making a hell of a row. The NCO got up, told them to stop or he would put them all on a charge. They rolled him up in a blanket, carried him out and threw him in the middle of a muddy pool. Then they came back in and locked the door.

When the Sergeant Major found out he laughed. "That's the finish of him. Didn't think he'd last long."

Although they were a rough lot, sang Sinn Fein songs, they didn't need training, could do anything with a rifle. And there was one sergeant the Irish did like. So for him they would put on their best drill, the best gunnery display ever seen in Harrogate. He was called Sergeant Gunn, and was strict but fair. But for any other sergeant the Irish simply didn't turn up, could never be found when it was time for parade. Apart from the Red Shield and the YMCA places, there were miles of lavatories in the camp. And if you stood on the lavatory seat, they couldn't see you when they looked under the door. Then, if you were quick and squatted on the floor, they couldn't see you when they looked through the window.

When the Irish had leave, they had to be given civilian clothing. Then the Sinn Fein half of them had to be caught before they would come back. Most of them were already deserters from the Irish Army. And though many of them were staunch Sinn Feiners, they would rather fight for the British than go back to Ireland. The discipline in the Irish Army was much harsher than in the British. If they had been sent to an Irish military prison they would have had their heads shaved the day they went in and again the day they came out.

Jim was put in their hut, in the bunk under Eddy. He was an Exmouth salmon fisherman. But, though they both came from Devon, Jim didn't talk to Eddy very much. Jim had to wear glasses, so he wasn't A1 like the rest. And he drank on his own. Eddy put him down as a real queer cove.

Sunday came.

"Always like this on a Sunday in here?" Jim asked Eddy. "Bloody rules is In Bed or Out Of Barracks. Not a bloody row like this."

"I shouldn't say bugger all," Eddy advised him. "With this lot you'd get a right bloody beating."

"Don't know about that," Jim said. "I ain't putting up with this."

Jim got out of his bunk. He was already stripped to the waist. His body was all hairy. He tied his braces around his trousers and put on his army boots.

"Want some bloody order in this place," he said to the Irish. The Irish stopped arguing.

"Tell you what," Jim said. "You're supposed to be hard, you Irish blokes. I'll fight the bloody lot of you. You come up one at a time."

Hawkins was from County Down. He was tall. He said to Eddy: "Jesus, your mate's asking for it."

"I dunno," Eddy said. "Think I'll push off. I don't mind a scrap, one against ..."

"I'll take you first, Burkee!" Jim shouted, and thump, he belted Burkee, knocked him flat and then kicked him, taking half his ear off.

"Understands you likes kicking," Jim said. "We does that down our way too."

Nolan was next. Then another. Jim laid into them, and laid them out. Jim was being knocked about, had a big cut down his back. Eddy thought he had better slip out and get the Sergeant Major. The Sergeant Major told the officer on duty.

"You'd better bring an ambulance," Eddy said.

When they got up to the barrack room, it was a shambles. But Jim was still standing, his back to the double doors. Ten or twelve of the Irish were laid out around him. The rest had thought better of it. They took the casualties to hospital. Jim had twenty stitches down his back. Burkee never came back. They made Jim NCO in charge of the barrack. The Irish thought the world of him.

The camp had a huge cookhouse – for eight thousand men, with two thousand ATS to look after them. Not one of the two thousand ATS girls could cook.

When Eddy was on guard his main job was clearing out men and women who were having a 'little bit' in the gunsheds. He would give them as long as he could, then go round the sheds shouting: "Come on! Knickers up! 'Way you go!" And he would hear them scuffling about behind the guns.

One day a detachment of Royal Marines arrived. They too were to be made into commando artillery, were to learn how to use the twenty-five-pounders.

The first day there, the Royal Marines sat down to eat with Eddy and the rest. When the officer came round to ask if there were any complaints, the Royal Marines all stood up like one man. And every single one of them made a complaint about the food. After that, their own cookhouse came. Eddy and the rest, though, had to go on suffering the ATS cooking.

The bread was always cut up and put in tea-chests. Above the tea-chests was a notice saying: 'Eat as much bread as you want'. One day Eddy was particularly hungry, and the food was repulsive. So he went to get himself some more bread, and some for his friends while he was there. An Irish ATS corporal came in and started calling him names for taking so much bread. Eddy picked her up and stuck her headfirst into one of the tea-chests, leaving her with her bum sticking up in the air and her legs kicking.

She was an NCO. Eddy was a gunner. She fell-in two men and before Eddy knew it, he was in the guardroom. He was brought in front of Richards – Gordon Richards they called him because he was the same size as the jockey. Eddy wasn't worried, knew that he would get away with it on two counts.

He knew that the sergeant knocked your hat off when you were brought up on a charge. Before going in to see the officer, the order was "Hats Off!" This one sergeant, however, didn't give anyone a chance to take their hat off themselves. He knocked it off. Just as he went to knock Eddy's hat off Eddy lifted his head and the sergeant smacked Eddy straight across the eyes. When Eddy got into the office, he could hardly see.

"What's the matter with your face?" Richards asked him.

"The sergeant struck me, Sir," Eddy said. The sergeant scowled at Eddy.

"Is that correct?" Richards asked the two escorts.

"Yes, Sir," they said.

"It was an accident, Sir," the Sergeant said. "I was knocking his hat off."

Richards wouldn't let the sergeant down, said that he would proceed with the case.

"Why did you assault the corporal?"

"Well, Sir," Eddy said, "I came into the Army to be managed by men, not to be called an effing so-and-so by a bloody Irish woman. Or a bloody English woman come to that. You can put me away for the rest of the war, but I'm not putting up with that. My wife wouldn't speak to me like that, and I'm bloody sure a slut like that isn't going to, either."

"Now, now, now," Richards said. "But she shouldn't have sworn at you. Case dismissed."

The clerk in the office told Eddy afterwards that the sergeant got a hell of a bollocking for hitting Eddy, told Eddy to keep to the other side of the barracks from him. The ATS corporal was going with another gunner – a scruffy little character from Glasgow. He was supposed to be hard. But nothing came of either. The camp was so big that their paths never crossed again.

A bank manager, a little man with glasses and in plus-fours, came up to the camp after bank hours to train them in unarmed combat. They also had a PE instructor they called Patterson and Celtic – Patterson was full back for Celtic Football Club. Most of the PE instructors were famous boxers or footballers.

One of the gunnery sergeants was from India. He did not like Eddy. One day he was showing them how to use an eighteen-pounder. There was no need for them to learn an eighteen-pounder: they would never be using one. On an eighteen-pounder, the shell was slapped up and then a heavy door, like an oven door, was slammed over it. Having slapped the shell up, that man then hit the barrel as a signal to the next man to slam the door. Eddy slapped the shell up. The sergeant didn't wait for Eddy's signal, slammed the door on Eddy's glove.

The fingers on the glove were stretched about six inches long. With his free hand, Eddy felt down his numb fingers.

"You bastard," Eddy said to the Sergeant. "You've taken the top of me bloody finger off."

Leaving the sergeant to be threatened with murder by the Irish, Eddy went down to the hospital. The nail and all the flesh had come off the top of the finger with just the bone sticking out. What was left of the quick of the nail looked like a piece of tissue paper. They built the flesh back up around the bone with some new Canadian stuff inside a silver case. A couple of ambulance men held him down while the stuff was rubbed on. It was like putting a white hot poker on the flesh. For five minutes after Eddy was let up, he was stuck with the same pained expression on his face. The next day there was a black scab where they had rubbed the stuff on.

As for the sergeant – he had put Eddy on a fizzer. He said that Eddy had threatened to hit him with an iron bar. The charge itself was the sergeant's undoing. The CO ignored the charge and asked what the hell the men had been doing training on an eighteen-pounder anyway.

"I thought it would be good training," the sergeant answered. No-one was allowed to think for themselves in the Army. Charge dismissed. And it was a long walk from the camp to the nearest pubs. The sergeant drank in a little village, a lonely place, by a bridge over a small river. The sergeant was found in the river one morning. He wasn't dead, but he had been knocked about a bit. It wasn't that the Irish particularly liked Eddy, more that they had particularly disliked that sergeant.

His training finished, Eddy was sent on embarkation leave. Just before he left, he had his teeth cleaned and scraped, and he was given a booster injection. He arrived in London about seven. By then, he was feeling very hot. In the carriage on the Devon train was a Yank, his buxom girlfriend, and an old boy with a raffia bag. Everything was blacked out. The train started.

"Where're you going?" Eddy asked the girl.

"Black Horse, Heavitree," she said.

"Oh I know that," Eddy said.

"I'm a barmaid there," she said. "And this is my GI boyfriend, Hank."

"D'you drink?" the old boy asked.

"Oh yes," Eddy said. "I don't mind a drink." The old boy had four bottles of whisky in the raffia bag. He poured Eddy a tumblerful.

The doctor who had given Eddy the injection had told him not to drink for twenty-four hours. By the time Eddy arrived in Newton station, he was paralytic. By a bit of luck, he met Jack Warren, the taxi driver. Jack usually had to meet an officer there at that time. The officer hadn't turned up; and, because Eddy was in uniform, Jack smuggled him home.

Eddy was bad.

While Eddy had been away, the Yanks had arrived in Ellacombe and had set up large marquees in Brewery Park. Most of the GIs were billeted in the surrounding houses. The council had tried to billet some in Vera's house. Ned had gone down to the council offices in Castle Circus and had raised hell – what were they trying to do, break up his daughter's marriage?

The first morning home, Eddy stayed on in bed while Vera went off to work. She was short-handed in the shop. Eileen had been called up, had gone to work on the buses; and Margaret had got herself in the family way.

Eddy was having a wash and a shave when there was a knock on the door. Ned had warned him that a man from the Town Hall was coming up to see him, had told Eddy not to give in to him.

"Good morning," Eddy said.

"Good morning. Glad I caught you in," the man said. "When are you going back?"

Now that really annoyed Eddy – whenever he came home on leave, and he met anyone, the first question they asked was when was he going back.

"I've come about your wife billeting some Americans."

"You've been here before haven't you?" Eddy said.

"I've seen your father-in-law."

"How'd you get on with him?"

"Not very well."

"How many Americans you got up your house?"

"That's no business of yours."

"Just as much business of mine if you mean to bring 'em in here. How many you got?"

"I haven't got any."

"You got a bloody big house up there." Eddy knew that he lived up the Warberrys. "And it'd be asking for trouble putting three or four Yanks in here with my wife on her own. I'm not having it." The man started to argue.

"I shouldn't argue," Eddy told him. "Or you'll be down over them steps."

While Eddy was on leave there was a Home Guard exercise. It was a beautiful misty morning. Eddy thought he would wander down and see the lads, say hello to Percy Bragg and Captain Dampier.

The Home Guard was all over Walls Hill and down Babbacombe. They were marching down behind the houses, creeping through the bushes. As Eddy was walking towards Anstey's Cove, he thought to himself – *just the time for Jerry to come in.* And no sooner had he thought it than – *Christ!* – he could hear the planes coming.

Vera had come to dread Eddy coming home. Because every time Eddy came home on leave there was a raid.

Now, Eddy did not know what to do – whether to lie in the road, run for it, or what. A plane came up over the Palace Hotel. In the drive to the Palace were two boys. They were seventeen, too young to go into the army. They were in the Chelston Home Guard. The plane dropped a bomb right on them.

Eddy jumped a five-foot stone wall. He pitched in beside Jack Fagin. Jack Fagin had been in the Great War. He was always drunk.

"Where the hell did you come from?" he yelled at Eddy. The bolt on his rifle was rattling.

"Over the bloody wall," Eddy said. "There's two poor buggers out there caught a packet."

The raid stopped. Eddy went on down the road. Part of the Palace Hotel had gone. At the top of a fire escape was a Women's Army Corps member. Half her face had been blown off. She was conscious. Her language was shocking. The Home Guard got up to her with a stretcher.

Captain Dampier said to Eddy: "I'm commandeering you. You take Shapley and this man, and you go up to the crater where the two boys were killed, and you don't let anyone up or down the road until the police arrive."

Jack Shapley was fat and bronchitic. He went wheezing up the road after Eddy.

Eddy had seen people who had been blown up in the blitz. There's a lot of muck on them and you can't really make out a body. Now he could just about make out what was left of the two boys in the crater. On top of the crater was a black bit of leggings and a boot.

"I don't see no bloody bodies," Jack Shapley said.

"What d'you think that is there?" Eddy said. Jack fainted and fell in the pit.

They hauled him out. Some fir branches had come down from a nearby tree. Eddy covered the remains with them. And it was not very long before the police turned up. It began to rain. The skies opened. Soon they were all soaking.

The bombs had killed fifty Polish Officers and some nurses who had been in the Palace Hotel. Many others were injured. They found one of the Polish officers alive a week afterwards down in the cellar. The Palace Hotel had been used as a hospital. There were red crosses painted on its roof.

"Trouble is," an officer said to Eddy, "soon as this lot get into operation again they'll bomb every hospital in sight in France. That's the trouble – one lot does it, and one thing leads to another."

Nine

April – May 1942

April 1942: Japanese make raids on Ceylon.

April 3rd 1942: Japanese bomb Mandalay.

April 5th 1942: 'Cornwall' and 'Dorsetshire' are sunk outside Colombo. 'Hermes' is sunk in Trincomalee. British fleet flees to Kenya.

April 9th 1942: Bataan and Philippines under Japanese control.

April 18th 1942: 'Hornet' attacks Tokyo

April 24th 1942: 'Baedecker' raids (reprisals for Lubeck) on Exeter, then Bath, then York.

April 27th 1942: 'Baedecker' raid on Norwich.

April 29th 1942: Burma road lost.

May 1st 1942: British troops retreat across River Chindwin.

May 3rd 1942: 'Baedecker' raid on Exeter.

May 4th-8th 1942: Battle of Coral Sea.

May 8th 1942: British take Madagascar from the Vichy French.

May 30th 1942: RAF obliterates 600 acres of Cologne. Midget submarine sinks 'Rumilles' in Diego Suazej harbour.

May 31st 1942: 'Baedecker' raid on Canterbury.

Eddy was sent to a big old estate near Hessle, seven miles from Hull. The estate had already been declared unfit for Italian prisoners. There was no hot water in the huts; the men had to wash outside in a trough. And they had to keep cutting trees down on the estate because they were dangerous. So did the commando part of his training begin.

There was an infantry assault course on the estate. First thing every Monday morning, with eight men to each twenty-five-pounder gun – Eddy was always on the bar because he was the tallest – they would complete a six to eight mile run around the town with it. Then they had to take it to a forest that had been cut down, through a village that had been bombed, let it down into a sandpit and pull it up the other side. It used to rupture more men than do them good. And on top of that they had to do the infantry assault course as well.

Vera started sleeping at her mother and father's. The council came up to say that they were going to requisition her house for evacuees because it was not being used. So Vera returned there to live; and she let out half the house to Muriel.

She did Muriel's hair. The man Muriel was to marry – Roy – worked in her father's bakery. The marriage was against her father's wishes. Vera did all the family's hair. Muriel told her that she and Roy couldn't get a flat, had nowhere to go. So Muriel and Roy became her tenants. Unbeknownst to Vera, Muriel was four months pregnant, hence her father's displeasure.

Eddy didn't like Roy, thought he was a pig. Eddy happened to be at home on the weekend they moved in, and Eddy had to help carry all Muriel's stuff up the path. Roy had just left her to it. Another weekend Roy thought that Eddy had gone back. But Eddy was upstairs, and he heard Roy shouting at Muriel about the doormats, which for some reason he had taken a dislike to. Eddy came down, told him that he had to go.

While Muriel and Roy had lived with her, because Roy got up early in the morning to go to the bakery, he and Muriel had gone to bed early. After they left, Vera discovered that they had kept the electric fire on in their room all evening every evening.

She next let her spare room to Florrie and her daughter Daphne. Florrie came from Hemel Hempstead. Her husband was in the army, came to visit her when he could – usually on those weekends when Eddy was also home.

Day and night, Eddy heard the bed going. Florrie's husband was about to join the 8th Army.

One Sunday, in the kitchen, he said to Eddy: "I got to go abroad. Cairo, Egypt."

"What are you trying to do?" Eddy asked him.

"Why?"

"You won't be fit to go to Aldershot, let alone Cairo." He had so worn himself out with Florrie he could hardly lift his arm.

"I don't trouble a bugger," he said. "They can grade me down. Mightn't get another chance."

In Hull, there was a gang of spivs and dead-end kids, made their living from the black market and thieving. They hung out in The Broadway. Eddy couldn't work out how they had all managed to stay out of the Army. They ran the town. Before Eddy's lot had arrived, they kicked a young soldier to death. They were always picking fights with soldiers. One day some of the sergeants decided to take whoever wanted to come and to go down and give them a hammering. Jim, the salmon fisherman, beat them to it.

The gang had a girl who started trouble for them. She wore her hair up in a bun. Eddy had stood behind her once, had seen the nits crawling through her hair.

Jim was a quiet man, liked to drink in peace. The girl picked on him. Jim punched her. Then he took on the rest.

With all the men away, Vera went to the occasional dance with Rene, Margaret and Eileen. Most of the men they danced with were soldiers, RAF men and Canadians.

Most evenings, though, they visited each others' houses, sometimes went for a drink down the Strand, or went up to Vera Toms at The Epicure for something under the counter.

In Hull there was a regular army man called Reg Norris. He came from Newton Abbot and was a gun artificer. He and his staff kept the guns in good condition.

The Sergeant Major was called The Bull. One day all the troops were lined up ready to march off – to go to the picture house in Hull. Eddy got called off. He tried to think what he could have done.

"I want to see you," The Bull said. "I see in your records you can play the drums."

"Yes," Eddy said.

"The drummer in our dance band here is shocking," The Bull said. "Bloody shocking."

"How much will I get?"

"A couple of pounds a week extra – playing in the Sergeants' Mess and at the boys' dance. Twice a week. Sometimes three times. There's a do tonight in the Sergeants' Mess. But if you play there, you keep your bloody eyes shut and your mouth shut. You see nothing." Eddy agreed.

Eddy passed his audition with flying colours. A couple of days later, Reg Norris came up to him. "You and I got to go'n see the Sergeant Major."

"Look," The Bull said to Eddy. "I'd like to keep you here in the dance band. You've passed all your laying tests?"

"Oh yes," Eddy said. "I've got A1 laying tests."

"Norris reckons you'd be alright as an instructor here. Instructing laying the guns. You'd be like a gun tiffy officer, not a repair bloke. And you'd be kept out, be here for the rest of the war. So we'll get you graded down to B1."

Eddy wrote home to tell Vera. All those who had been with him and had passed were sent on to Watford. Watford was a big holding centre.

Three days after Eddy had written to Vera, a new order arrived. Everybody in Hull had to have a new medical. They had been twigged. There were too many A1 men there who had been falsely graded down. Eddy never even got to his medical: he was still A1 plus.

"My Christ," The Bull said. "We're going to have a big turnout here." Reg Norris was alright – he had been awarded the Military Medal for staying behind at Dunkirk to spike six guns. He stayed. Eddy was sent on to Watford on his own.

Ten

June 1942

June 2nd 1942: 'Baedecker' raid on Canterbury.
June 4th 1942: USA victorious in battle of Midway.
June 6th 1942: 'Baedecker' raid on Canterbury.
June 21st 1942: Tobruk taken by Rommel (33,000 troops captured). Auchinleck defends El Alamein. 'Baedecker' raid on Norwich.

In Watford it was like going for a job each day. Mornings and afternoons Eddy, along with two thousand other troops, had to go up to the square behind the cinema. A sergeant major shouted out that so many anti-tank gunners were wanted. Nobody moved. So many infantrymen. Nobody moved. The sergeant major was Irish.

"Bejasus, what a bastard lot. Nobody's been trained as an anti-tank gunner. Nobody's been trained as infantry. Right! You, you, you, you, you and you."

Eddy found himself volunteered for Burma. He had to go to one end of Watford and draw a pith helmet, then down to the other end of town for his tropical uniform, his shorts and his long socks, then back across town again ... until his kit bag was full. Then, when he went down to the station with the rest bound for Burma, he was called off. So he had to go to the far end of town to return the pith helmet, then back across town to return his tropical uniform, and so on. That happened twice.

The sergeant major told Eddy that he wouldn't be going anywhere for a while – because he had been recommended as an NCO, he'd passed his laying tests, the special medical had qualified him for the commandos, and he was earmarked for a War Office regiment. Mornings and afternoons, however, he still had to go up to the square.

"The only time I see any action," Eddy told the men in his billet, "is when I go home on leave."

Evenings, Vera read. Her mother read Pamela Ayres, Barbara Cartland and Elinor Glyn. Elinor Glyn's heroes were always handsome with a straight nose. Vera's taste tended more to historical novels – Geoffery Farnell and Daphne du Maurier. When Eddy was home, he read Zane Grey. Like Vera, he enjoyed Geoffery Farnell's books – about old prize fighters and highwaymen.

Most evenings, Vera listened to Radio Luxembourg, on Sundays to It's That Man Again and the Crazy Gang. Ned waited up every night to listen to Lord Haw Haw telling the British how many planes they'd lost, how many ships, how many men ...

"Hello. This is Germany calling. Germany calling ..."

"You liar!" Ned shouted at the radio.

"Why do you listen to it," Vera's mother asked him, "if it's only a lot of lies?"

But every midnight, Ned would be there at the radio.

"This is Lord Haw Haw speaking ..."

"Liar!"

One of the Watford sergeants had been badly wounded in the desert. There was a big scar down one side of his face. He thought all the men in Watford were shirkers, was a bit of a bastard to them. They only had one gun in Watford. The sergeant would get all the gunners down on that gun to keep their eye in.

One day he said: "Anybody lay a gun?"

Eddy said to a bloke called Johnstone: "Say yes. Go on."

"Why?" Nobody volunteered anything in the army.

"Say yes. Go on," Eddy nudged him: both of them were layers. "Yes, we can lay Sergeant."

"Oh. That's the first person to speak up," the Sergeant said. "Never knew any of you buggers could lay anything. I can't even get 'em to say they're gunners."

Eddy and Johnstone went through the procedures, laid the gun, picked out a clock tower as API. It was easy once you knew how.

"Right," the sergeant said. "I don't want to see you two anymore. You just go up and sign on mornings and afternoons. If you aren't posted, do what you like for the rest of the day."

Eddy and Johnstone had it made, spent their days in the Red Shield while the other poor buggers had to go round and round the town pulling the gun. And, until he got another gun, the sergeant had them doing it in relays.

In Vera's shop the ceilings stayed down, the curtains were in tatters, but it was business as usual. Except when they had a power cut. And the power cuts always came without warning. So for two hours or more there would be customers sitting around with wringing wet hair, or waiting to finish the second half of their perms.

One customer was a miserable trout, always moaning. She was old-fashioned, fussy about her hair. Vera was always on at her to have it done a bit more modern.

One day she came in and said: "I'll let you do what you want with it." So Vera restyled her hair. Next time she came in, she had a bit of lipstick on.

Vera said to Rene: "I bet you a hundred thousand pounds she's got a fancy man."

"Never!" Rene said. "Who'd have her?" Her husband was away in the Navy.

The next time she came in she couldn't stop talking, had to tell someone. She told Vera. The fancy man was an American, and he was called Buck. Soon after that, Vera saw her with him. Buck was a big man, tall and handsome. And black. From then on every time she had her hair done Vera heard all about what he had given her.

"What else? What else?" Rene would poke Vera. The whole shop knew, passing it on to one another. Vera encouraged her to tell more.

"Oh how lovely. What else?" Soon she was telling Vera how he made love to her, how she'd never been made love to like that before, how different they were to Englishmen, how he would hang it out so that she could have 'a thrill'. She had never had 'a thrill' with her husband, but Buck used to hold on for her; and his was twice as big as her husband's and mauve on the end. And while Vera was being told all this, she could hear the girls in the shop behind her desperately trying not to laugh.

One day the sergeant major said to Eddy: "I want you clean perfect tomorrow. Brasses inside and out. Press everything. You're going for an interview. You and a Welsh bloke." Half the men Eddy had trained with had already left for their commando regiments.

"Interview?" Eddy said.

"Yes. Interview. Hear what I said?" Sergeants never explained anything.

Eddy cleaned up and went down to the battery office. The insides of his braces were inspected. No soldier was ever told that he was perfectly turned out, always a little fault was picked. Eddy was then marched in to see Colonel Fenshaw. Colonel Fenshaw stuttered a bit. He examined Eddy's records.

"I see you've passed three laying tests?"

"Yes, Sir."

"You've never laid self-propelled guns?"

"No, Sir. Never seen one."

"And you missed the infantry ... Oh yes. You'll do. I'll have you."

None the wiser, Eddy went outside. The Welsh bloke came out. He was an OPAck, did the brainy part of gunnery, worked out everything in logarithms – how long it would take the shell to get there according to the wind and the weather. He had passed too. Three days later they were sent to Codford on Salisbury Plain.

Eleven

July 1942 – March 1943

August 1942: Churchill dismisses Auchinleck, replaces him with General Alexander. Commander of 8th Army now Montgomery.
August 7th 1942: Battle of Guadalcanal begins.
August 19th 1942: Allies raid Dieppe, lose 6,000 troops. RAF 'Pathfinder' force created. Russians defending Stalingrad.
August 21st 1942: USA victorious in Battle of Tonane River.
September 13th 1942: USA victorious in Battle of Bloody Ridge.
October 12th 1942: USA victorious in Battle of Cape Esperance.
October 23rd 1942: Montgomery attacks Rommel at El Alamein.
October 26th 1942: USA victorious in Battle of Santa Cruz Islands.
November 2nd 1942: Montgomery's second attack on Rommel.
November 4th 1942: Rommel in retreat from Egypt.
November 8th 1942: Allied troops land in Morocco and Algiers, move into Tunis.
November 10th 1942: Churchill's speech '... the end of the beginning'.
November 15th 1942: British church bells are rung to celebrate Montgomery's victory. Japanese victorious in Battle of Tansafaronga Point.
December 1st 1942: Beveridge Report published.

January 2nd 1943: Allies take Burma. Churchill and Roosevelt meet in Casablanca. Germans start to retreat from Russia.

January 30th 1943: Japanese evacuated from Gaudalcanal.

January 31st 1943: German Stalingrad forces surrender (92,000 prisoners).

February 1943: Rommel retreats to Tunisia.

February 7th 1943: Kursk taken by Russians.

February 11th 1943: Lozoraya taken by Russians.

February 16th 1943: Kharkov taken by Russians.

March 3rd & 4th 1943: Japanese lose Battle of the Bismarck Sea.

March 5th 1943: Essen bombed.

March 8th 1943: 173 killed in Bethnal Green Tube Station.

March 15th 1943: Russians lose Kharkov. Orde Wingate has first successes in Burma.

The regiment Eddy had to join at Codford was the Hertfordshire Yeomanry. It had been a Territorial regiment, was now a War Office regiment of artillery commando. There were only four War Office regiments in the whole army. Being a War Office regiment meant that they were more independent than most.

Three Scotsmen were moved into Eddy's hut. The first fortnight, Eddy was on every fatigue going. Company Sergeant Major Barlowe had been with the Terriers. He was over forty. In civvy street, he had been a bus cleaner. He was good on the guns though.

After a fortnight Eddy said to him: "Excuse me Sergeant Major, I know my name's easy, but I've been on all the fatigues."

"What about it?" Sergeant Major Barlowe had a sad face. They called him 'Dad'.

"I don't mind my share but..."

"But your name's so easy. Dart. Comes out easy. Right? The other buggers are called Macfarlane and Macthis and Macthat."

All Sergeants fancied themselves humorists. Dad was no different. Eddy being called Dart, he was again dubbed Double-top.

One night a girl was raped. On the way home from a village dance some soldier had caught hold of her and had beaten her up as well as raping her. The police brought her up to the camp to identify the soldier. Her face was black and blue, her eyes swollen, her nose broken. They put her in a wheelchair to go along the ranks of the Hertfordshire Artillery Commando, the Essex Yeomanry, the Pioneers and another regiment. Four regiments in all, about twenty-thousand men.

Three civilian policemen and five redcaps accompanied her as she was wheeled up and down the ranks of the men at attention. She stopped and looked at every man's face, officers included.

Every man felt guilty.

After a couple of hours, with no hesitation at all, she picked out a man in the Pioneers. The redcaps got him away quick – before the men could turn on him. And the girl wasn't mistaken: the man had scratches on him; he confessed.

Eddy was at Codford for three weeks. On the weekend that Vera was to visit him, he was transferred.

Ned had diarrhoea in the middle of a raid.

"Come in! Come in!" Vera and her mother called him. Reluctantly, Ned left the outside lavatory and ran indoors to the shelter. At that moment, there was a huge bang.

After the all-clear, they went out to inspect the damage. The lavatory door was in splinters. A cannon shell had gone through the lavatory wall, through Mac's next door, and had ended up at Bert Ewens'. If Ned hadn't moved, the shell would have gone through his stomach.

"The sods," he said. "That could've hit me. Look!" Ned took it personally.

Eddy was sent to Poole in Dorset. The guns were there. He hadn't been on a real gun yet. They wanted a waiter in the Sergeants' Mess. Eddy wasn't fussy. There was a Totnes bloke already in there. The Totnes bloke had been in every detention you could think of. Eddy liked being a waiter – he was getting double food; and the food in the Sergeants' Mess was better than in the Officers' Mess. But it was too good to last. One day they collared him out of there and sent him out to sea on a self-propelled gun.

They had old Matilda tanks fitted with twenty-five-pounders. The Matildas had a square turret with two doors at the back. The first four men who had fired the gun had been killed by the blast. After that they kept the doors open when they fired.

Each barge had four guns. The deck had split on the first barge that all four had fired from. After that, they built barges hinged in the centre. In a rough sea, the barges tended to whip when they hit a trough. Men were sent out in them to get their sea legs. But, although Eddy had been sick in rowing boats before, he was not sick on the barge.

The guns were shackled to the deck of the barge. Eddy was put on the front gun. This being another first time, no-one knew quite what would happen until they fired. They were to practise in Studland bay. The captain of the barge had a Coventry Clock. He set it to keep the gunners on line with the target – the Coventry Clock acting as GAP1. As they closed, they would have to reduce their range. That meant changing the range cones on the shells. They would fire fifty, reduce one hundred yards, fire fifty. Speed was of the essence; and so it would be a bit of a bugger because of the Matildas' open turret doors getting in the way. And the Matildas had a limited trajectory. It wasn't so bad their being fixed on the barges, but on land the driver would have to shift the tank, and the tank had to go the opposite way to the target. If the aimer wanted to shift right, the tank went left, and vice versa. Eddy had done none of this before.

Everyone was told to put on steel helmets. When the two forward guns fired, all the electric light fittings came off the bulkheads and bits of iron popped up everywhere. When the two rear guns fired they nearly took the forward gunners' heads off.

With that experiment unsuccessful, the Hertfordshire Yeomanry of commando artillery was sent running around Hampshire. Then they were put on a train to Scotland, ended up in Invernary, between Kilmarnock and Ayr.

Most of the regiment was billeted in a large manor house with spacious grounds. Eddy's battery was put in a Nissen hut on a hill. One day, as an exercise, they all had to climb some ropes up a cliff. Dad Barlowe made it to the top but many of the younger men did not.

On the way to Scotland they had picked up some Yankee 105-millimeter self-propelled guns called Priests. Two men manned them. One was a layer for the range, and the other was a layer on the dial sight. Their guns didn't go in degrees like the British. So the gunners had to consult a table that converted their measurements into degrees. It was a hell of a job. They had to fire range cones. As they went down from the longest range – the most powerful – Eddy had to whip off the range cone and shove on another.

The regiment practiced until they got the hang of them. Then the War Office ordered them to drive the guns as hard as they could. The Priests had rubber tracks. All over Scotland they went, over every battle range, up sunken roads, over moors ... The gunners were covered in bruises.

One day Churchill, Montgomery and some other nobs came up to watch them have a big shoot, see how they were getting on with the guns. Spud's baby was born that day. Churchill found out and ordered one round each for a twenty-one gun salute.

"There you are," Churchill told Spud. "You can tell your son when he grows up that Churchill ordered a twenty-one gun salute to be fired in his honour."

"Yes, that's alright," Spud said. "But I'll want something to prove it, Sir."

"I'll bloody well write it out for you," Churchill said, and did.

The rubber tracks of the Priests were worn out within three months.

Twelve

April 1943 – April 1944

April 6th 1943: Burma – British troops routed in Arakan Campaign.

May 12th 1943: Rommel beaten. Attu taken by Allies.

May 16th 1943: 'Dambusters' destroy Möhne and Eder dams.

May 29th 1943: Barman-Wappertal destroyed by RAF. Washington conference.

June 1943: Ribbentrop and Molotov meet to unsuccessfully discuss peace terms. 61,000 Allied POWs building Burma railway.

July 9th 1943: Allies land in Sicily.

July 24th-29th 1943: Hamburg bombed.

July 25th 1943: Benito Mussolini replaced by Marshal Badoglio.

August 1943: 130 killed in tip-and-run raid on Plymouth.

August 5th 1943: Russians take Orel and Belgorod.

August 12th-13th 1943: First V1s (Doodlebugs/Buzz Bombs) land in S E England.

August 15th-16th 1943: V1 attacks, day and night.

August 18th 1943: Allies take Sicily. Marshal Badoglio sues for peace.

August 23rd 1943: Russians take Kharkov.

September 2nd 1943: Allies land at Taranto.

September 3rd 1943: Allies land at Reggio.

September 8th 1943: Allies and Italians announce agreement (Germans in Italy continue fighting).

September 9th 1943: Allies land at Salerno.

September 11th 1943: Salamanca taken by the Australians.

September 16th 1943: Lae taken by the Australians.

September 25th 1943: Smolensk taken by the Russians.

November 1943: Another tip-and-run raid on Plymouth. Sir Oswald Mosley released from prison. Burma railway completed. Tarawara taken by Allies. The bombing of Berlin begins (continues until March 1944).

December 1943: Churchill contracts pneumonia in North Africa. A winter of strikes. Allies gain control of Vitiaz Straits. First use of Mustangs as bomber escorts.

January 3rd 1944: Russians take Norvigral Volynsk.

January 21st 1944: 'Little Blitz' begins on London (continues through to March 1944).

February 5th 1944: Russians take Rovno.

February 8th 1944: Russians take Nikopol.

February 12th 1944: 'Khedive Ismail' troopship sunk, 1,000 troops lost.

February 25th 1944: Schweinfurst bombed.

March 13th 1944: Russians take Khersen.

March 18th 1944: 72 Allied prisoners beheaded aboard 'Tone'. Germans occupy Hungary.

The regiment had been in Saxmunden before Eddy had joined it. Silly Suffolk they called it.

Eddy's lot were billeted in Warbleswick, opposite Southwold. Warbleswick was an artists' village; and those, who weren't artists or toffs, were locals all with the same name. It had a beach, a common and woods. On the common were the burial grounds of ancient Britons and nearby were swamps with masses of bullrushes.

All the ammunition was dumped in the woods on the heath. They had twenty-four guns. Each gun had eight hundred rounds, not counting smoke shells. With that lot dumped on their doorstep, and with air raids every night, the soldiers weren't too popular with the villagers. They wouldn't speak to the troops. The troops were none too happy themselves about having to sit on all that ammunition.

The American Priest guns were sent away for repair and renewal. That meant that the commando artillery of the Hertfordshire Yeomanry had again to do infantry training. Stripped to the waist, they ran through the swamps. Eddy came upon low cottages in the woods that belonged back in King Alfred's time. There'd be a few pigs, pigeons and chickens; and the whole family would come out and watch the soldiers run past. The troops also did a lot of boxing training and unarmed combat.

After the first few nights, the men refused to go on guard alone on the common. Especially the Scottish Highlanders – they were very superstitious. The common was weird, creepy. Locals would appear right behind the soldiers and the soldiers didn't hear them coming. It was about two miles around the perimeter of the compound. Mackenzie wouldn't go on his own: Eddy had to go with him.

"It's only wind or something," Eddy said. "I'm not really worried. Shoot the bastards anyhow if they come up too close." But that night they never saw anyone.

Warbleswick became the only place where the men were allowed to patrol in pairs. Major Swann tried to change this. He asked Eddy to be the first to patrol on his own.

"I'm not all that keen on it, Sir."

"If we've got to have two men, then we've got to have two men. But I'd like you to give it a go and see. You're not afraid are you?"

"Well, I come from near Dartmoor," Eddy said. "And they're just as superstitious down there."

Eddy got on well with Swanny, so he went out on his own. He was terrified, put a round up the spout. All the time it was as if someone was walking about twenty yards behind him. When Eddy stopped, the footsteps following him stopped. When he walked on the heather, they also walked on the heather. He couldn't see anyone, and there was no cover.

On finishing his patrol he went to Swanny's quarters in the village to report to him.

"My God, you're white," Swanny said.

"I'm frightened stiff," Eddy told him. "Wish you could walk around with me, Sir."

"I don't bloody want to walk round with you. Here, have a Scotch."

Eddy liked Swanny – he never stood on rank, had given Eddy a Scotch even though he knew that Eddy was on duty. He also relented on the idea of men patrolling Warbleswick alone. They continued to patrol in pairs.

The troops were billeted in the artists' and toffs' houses. They were beautiful houses, had woodblock floors; and, when they got to know the artists and toffs a bit better, they were told about the locals. They said that they were always up on the common, believed in spirits. Eddy wasn't too sure if they were pulling his leg or not. They told him that in the house where he was billeted a man had hanged himself up in the roof ...

They were supposed to be seven to a crew on each gun. More often it was five, sometimes six. Eddy slept with his crew in a big attic dormer. The angle of the roof was boarded over and a door led into it so that a man could walk around inside. The man who'd hanged himself was supposed to have done it from a beam in there.

One night, before they went to bed, one of the men crept inside the roof and started moaning and tapping. Mackenzie was a hardcase, but superstitious. He started trembling, almost fainted. He went and asked for a transfer to another gun rather than sleep in that room.

Back in Devon, Mr Bucklett was in the part-time Fire Brigade. He was also the window cleaner. He came down Congella cleaning the windows. Ned was digging Eddy's garden.

Ned looked upon it as his part of the war effort to look after the gardens of all the men in the terrace who were in the services.

In the course of conversation Mr Bucklett said to Ned: "Them silly buggers that's gone in the services is bloody daft."

Ned had a rake in his hand. He said to Mr Bucklett: "You take that bloody bastard bucket, and that bloody cloth, and don't let me see you down this road again or I'll put this bloody rake through you." Mr Bucklett never returned, lost every single customer in Congella.

They never got the Priest guns back. The War Office decided that they should have Canadian Ram guns instead – they used British ammunition. So all the ammunition for the Yankee guns had to go. The Canadian Rams had Whirlwind Parker aero engines. They did two miles to the gallon.

They were returned to Scotland to train on the new guns. With masses of infantry, they took part in battle courses on the Isle of Booth. The barges they had used in Poole came up to Scotland. The gun crews kept to the same barges, trained on the lochs.

The captain of Eddy's barge was an old seadog, a hard man. The rest of the crew had ended up on the barge only after being thrown off every other kind of ship. The discipline was vastly different to that of a battleship.

On the last Liberty boat at half past eleven, for instance, it went right down to the gunwales, there were that many men on it. The man in charge of the Liberty boat had the final say as to who came aboard his boat, even above the officers. There being too many in the boat the barge crews said: "Chuck the Pongos off." Which was Eddy and the other soldiers. An officer reprimanded them. So they told the skipper of the Liberty boat to chuck the officer off. They didn't care; and, singing the Red Flag, they were taken back to their barges.

The crewman who worked the Bofors on Eddy's barge had two razor scars down either cheek from a scrap in Liverpool. The captain came from Weymouth, had run the gauntlet in Dunkirk, had run supplies into Tobruk, and was always three parts cut.

One day the captain said to Eddy: "What do you use that diesel for?" Eddy had four barrels of diesel, mixed it with the paint when they painted the guns. They were always painting the guns – brown. The diesel made the job quicker.

"Nothing really, Sir," Eddy said.

"You couldn't accidentally bust one or two? Let 'em run over the deck?"

"Could be done, Sir." Eddy wanted to keep in with him.

"I'll get them bloody yobboes of mine to scrub the decks. Bloody rusty, isn't they?" The crew were none too pleased with Eddy when they had to brush up the diesel.

The barge crew slept in the small galley. Eddy and four limber gunners slept in the even smaller storeroom under the bridge. They nailed some planks around a table for two of them to sleep on, and the rest slept on the deck. They had to be careful being under the bridge because the Captain always went for a piss sometime in the night, and by then his aim wasn't so good.

Every man had to take his turn in the barge galley. Few could cook. Eddy didn't go in the galley, was too artful for that. He had a limber gunner called Slapsy-Maxy, from Sheffield. He was a proper comedian, always laughing, always making up little ditties about people. And he was a good cook.

"Your turn in the galley next week, Slapsy," Eddy said to him. "Turn out some good grub. Tell you what, if the old man wants you to stay in the galley, would you be willing?"

"I don't mind," Slapsy said. He liked cooking.

"I'll clean your gun for you," Eddy said, knowing that the arrangement was totally against regulations. "I got bugger all else to do."

After Slapsy had been in the galley three days, Eddy was called to the bridge. Cap off, Navy fashion, he went in to see the captain.

"Who's this bloke in the galley then?" Eddy was asked.

"One of my gun crew, Sir."

"I never had grub like it."

"No Sir. He's a marvellous cook."

"He wouldn't consider staying there I suppose?"

"It's against regulations, Sir," Eddy said.

"I'll worry about that. None of us are likely to tell anyone."

"I'll have a word with him, Sir."

Eddy went to see Slapsy then reported back to the captain.

"He don't mind staying there all the time. So long as I clean his gun."

"Right. You're on," the captain said. "You'll get our razor and cigarette ration. For all the crew." The Navy got better rations than the Army, bought their own food from Navy shore bases like HMS Turtle.

The gunners' rations were delivered in big tea-chests. The barge crew threw all the gunners' rations overboard except for the bread, cheese and sugar. The gunners paid the barge crew a shilling a week and in return they were having things like raspberries and condensed milk while the rest of the Army ate bully beef.

The Germans bombed Exeter, Teignmouth, Dawlish, Exmouth, Dartmouth and Galmpton – anywhere where there were small boatyards. Torquay was on their list.

On Sunday, May 30th, Ned was lying under a tree on the lawn watching the ack-ack and the Focke-Wolfes. A bomb hit the church in St Marychurch. Twenty seven children and two teachers were killed.

When Ned heard, he wept.

In Ayr, Eddy took part in another exercise to see how many troops and vehicles could be moved into a certain area. They did other exercises in Stirling. Then more back in Ayr. In Kilmarnock, nearby, every other woman for miles around was suddenly wearing a coat made out of Army blankets.

Pete Hornet was a Cockney and a rogue. Somehow he and another man had waylaid a consignment of blankets.

"Who are these bastards flogging blankets in Kilmarnock?" the Besom, RSM Leftbridge, asked Eddy.

"Dunno, Sarge. How would I know?"

"Well, Hornet's your mate. Or isn't he? And you go in any pub, there's a woman wearing one of 'em."

And lovely coats they made – at least a thousand of them. But, although he was Pete Hornet's friend, Eddy never discovered how he had acquired the blankets.

Eddy took some RAF officers out on the gun, gave them a rough ride over the moors. In return they took Eddy and his crew up in their plane from Prescott. To pay them back for the rough ride they looped the loop. That was in a small plane. Another gun crew was taken up in a transport plane, found themselves out over the Irish Sea without a fighter escort.

One Saturday, Eddy and the other gunners went to a dance in the Wheatsheaf in Dunnoon. All the gunners were commando fit. They were invited to the dance by the local boys. The dancing was all Scottish reels. They did the Eightstone Reel, the Bonny Prince Charley ... and they went on and on ... Four bagpipes, two trumpets, hogsheads of beer and masses of whisky. The locals had supplied the booze – as much as they could drink. And still they danced. The commandos were all exhausted. The local boys carried on.

"Bloody hell," the Besom said. He had a voice like sawing wood – "Eighteen pints and still walk the line," was his boast in the mess.

"Bloody hell," he said this night. "This is what they ought to train the commandos on. Don't need nothing else."

From Scotland they returned to Saxmunden in Silly Suffolk; and from Suffolk they were sent to Norfolk.

They did an exercise in Norfolk – in a place chosen because it was remarkably similar to somewhere in Normandy. Because of the number of civilians living close by, the gunners had to be very accurate.

The regiment was based now in Norwich. They parked up to eight self-propelled guns at a time in the narrow, terraced streets. Each self-propelled gun weighed forty-two tons. After one week, the roads were torn up. The old people were terrified, especially when they did drill.

"Load! Seventy rounds gunfire! Fire!" The old people would stare at the guns outside their front doors and, trembling, wait for the bang. But it was only practise.

They had to take over some houses in Norwich, do them up. Eddy was there for Christmas 1943. A woman asked four of them to spend it at her house, near the YMCA.

One morning Eddy looked at orders and saw that he was down for a cadre course for eight weeks. At four thirty every morning he had to get up for that training, apart from having to do his normal duties afterwards. The Besom took them through the course, made them run everywhere. When the eight weeks were up they were all sent for an exam.

Eddy was right marker for the regiment – that meant that he was the first called out and the battery fell in on him. For the exam parade they all had to bring a pencil, show it in their breast pocket. Eddy Edwards didn't have one.

"Where's your pencil, Edwards?" the Besom asked him.

"Couldn't get one, Sarge."

"That's no excuse. If I tell you to bring a bloody monkey on your shoulder tomorrow morning you'll be here with a bloody monkey on your shoulder!"

One of the men on the exam parade had been in college, a trainee dental surgeon. He had only one more exam to pass to qualify. And Mackessock, from Scotland, had two more exams to pass to become a full blown doctor. The authorities had conscripted them both anyway.

The trainee dentist was so tall that he had to have two beds. They called him Drainpipe. He was a wizard with geometry. Before they went in to the exam, the Besom took Eddy to one side, asked him what Drainpipe was like.

"Clever, is he?"

"Could do the exam stood on his head. I can't do the algebra stuff, but I can do the puzzles. He can't do them." Eddy had been on an OPAck course.

"I can't do any of it," the Besom said. "The Army didn't want all that when I joined." The Besom had come from the original

Yeomanry regiment. "You'd better take my paper and see that it's done."

Inside the exam room the Besom slipped Eddy the paper. Eddy did part of it, Drainpipe the rest. Drainpipe did about twelve papers altogether. All of them passed top grade as potential NCOs.

Back in Norwich young Jock Mcloughlin caught mumps and had to be left behind when the regiment moved back to Poole.

With the first doodlebug rockets coming over, Vera could no longer depend on the air-raid wardens ringing Maison Vee's with a warning. Their warnings had been too late anyway. So, as before, she had to arrange it so that one girl was always standing in the shop doorway, not deafened by the driers, to listen for the sirens. Or, more likely, for the doodlebugs before the sirens.

Back in Poole the gun crews started exercises on the barges once again. But at least the decks had been reinforced. Eddy was on the 303 flotilla. His was always the last boat out of the harbour.

The regiment was billeted in Bournemouth, in all the lovely houses on the up-market side of town, their guns parked in the road. The first night there they got up at four o'clock in the morning and drove their guns to Poole in the dark for practise on the barges.

A barge carried four guns, shackled. There were four limber gunners, one NCO and one Bombardier to each gun. They practised about once a week.

When the barge wasn't taking the guns out, it took infantry out to get them used to being seasick. The barges had flat bottoms, had been made to bend in the middle, and whipped unpredictably in a rough sea.

"Not that lot again," the crew would say. "We'll have to hose the bloody deck down."

The Captain on the barge was good to the gunners. One day a Jimmy – a naval officer – joined the barge. The gunners were all playing cards in the small galley. On the barge they came under naval regulations. The Jimmy booked all the gunners for playing cards.

Being on a charge meant they would all have to go to HMS Turtle – the Navy barracks outside Poole. Eddy went to see the captain.

"He's a bloody twat," the captain said. "Can't run this boat like a destroyer. I've got to be careful though. I'm trying to talk some sense into him. The only thing I've got across to him so far is that someone'll chuck him overboard one night." The Jimmy got transferred.

Vera sent Eddy a pair of kid gloves. One afternoon he was in the Red Shield in Bournemouth alongside about ten French-Canadians. One of them was a full-blooded Red Indian scout. A loner. Eddy liked him, but not the other buggers. An evil lot, who all carried knives.

Eddy had put his gloves on the table beside his drink. Out of the corner of his eye, he saw the Canadian next to him pick up his gloves and pass them on to the next one. Eddy resigned himself to the idea that it was safer to say nothing.

But about half an hour later, Snowy White arrived. He was from Eddy's regiment; rough, Welsh, and as mad as a hatter. Then Snowy's Yorkshire friend came in with another from his regiment. All three were hardcases and they sat beside Eddy.

"See these buggers," Eddy said quietly to them. "They pinched the new gloves my missus sent me. There was too many of them for me to say anything by myself. Now you three's here, though, we'll have a go if you like."

"You got to watch their bloody knives," one of them warned. Eddy didn't tell them he had a knife in his puttee.

The Yorkshireman grunted. He got up and went around the back of the Canadians as if making to go out. Catching hold of three of them he banged their heads together. Then he got hold of another two by their ears. And they all piled in. Eddy got his gloves back, but they were not allowed in the Red Shield any more.

After that, he had to keep an eye out for the French-Canadians. Though his friend, the Indian, a whippy sinewy man, one night cleared all ten of them out of there after they turned on him.

Another night Eddy saw a Spanish Pioneer have a go at the Canadians. Eddy didn't see how it started, but he saw the Spanish Pioneer finish it. And there were three or four against him too. There were many Spaniards in the Pioneer Corps – big handsome buggers with long sideburns and very popular with the girls.

One of the crew on the barge was Scottish.

"Where were you the other night?" Eddy asked him one day. "I saw you in Poole. You were the only sailor there."

"That's right," he answered. "You know that cross-eyed girl in the pub? The one who keeps singing 'I wish I had a paper doll'?"

"Yes?" Eddy said.

"Well she looked bloody terrible to begin the evening. But the more I drank the better she looked. When I woke up in the morning, saw her beside me – frightened me out of my life."

After Poole, they went to Norwich, then Winchester, and then the New Forest. Between Romsey and Winchester, Eddy got a letter from Vera saying that she was pregnant.

Thirteen

April 1944: Allies bomb Budapest, Bucharest and Ploesti.

April 5th 1944: Russians take Razdelnaya.

April 10th 1944: Russians take Odessa.

April 17th 1944: Russians reach Sevastopol.

April 18th 1944: Last of 'Little Blitz'.

May 11th 1944: General Alexander begins offensive against Monte Cassino.

May 12th 1944: USAAF starts attacking oil dumps in Germany.

May 13th 1944: Russians take Crimea.

May 18th 1944: Monte Cassino falls.

May 27th 1944: First kamikaze raids in Battle for Biak.

June 2nd 1944: Flying-fortress shuttle service begins between Italy and Russia.

June 4th 1944: Allies enter Rome.

In the New Forest, apart from the Hertfordshire Yeomanry, there were US Rangers, the East Yorks, the Green Howards and the Durham Light Infantry. The Durham Light and the Green Howards had been through the war in the North African desert and the landings on Sicily. They considered Eddy's lot to be scum. No-one in the 8th Army thought that anyone but the Desert Rats were any good, and didn't pal up with anyone outside their own regiments.

Eddy's troop was camped in the woods near Romsey on Mountbatten's estate. During the day they had to stay under the trees to avoid detection from the air. Apart from that they could do what they liked in the New Forest, except leave it. The tanks and the guns had to be kept under cover, and could only be parked on roads where there was enough cover from trees alongside them. The NAAFIs were in big marquees under trees. They also had big camouflage nets stretched between trees. Nights were dangerous because the Germans were still raiding Southampton and spent anti-aircraft shells and shrapnel fell on the New Forest.

Eddy's regiment had Americans cooking for them. Most were from the South and were supposed to be unfit for active service, although they were all big men.

While in the New Forest the self-propelled guns were waterproofed so that, providing the driver could keep the engine going, the gun could be driven in up to eight feet of water.

Eddy's three friends were single. Unauthorised, they took a seventy-two-hour leave, booked up with three prostitutes in London, and buggered off. They'd been trained to get out of places. They left a note for Major Swann: 'Dear Sir, We're going to have our seventy-two hours and a bit of dick, then we'll be back.' The Major did nothing: they were all key men. When they got back they were sent to dig a trench outside the cookhouse.

Eddy thought about Vera being pregnant. He took her letter to show Dad Barlowe, the Company Sergeant Major.

"What's the procedure," Eddy asked him, "if I want seventy-two hours' leave?"

"You'll be bloody lucky."

"My wife's going to have a baby."

"Three parts of the invasion force's wives are going to have babies."

"Well I'm asking you what the procedure is."

"The procedure is you'll have to write a note to me first. When you've done that I'll pass it on to the second lieutenant. Then you've got to write a request to him, and he'll tell the first lieutenant. Then you write a request to him – when you get the word – and he'll write to the captain. Then you write a request to the captain. He'll tell Major Swann, and you'll write a request to him."

"I'm going on this leave, you know," Eddy told Dad Barlowe. "I can get to Torquay without getting on any train, don't you worry. I'll do what Spud Edwardes and the others did – I'll just tell Swanny that I'm going."

"Then," Dad continued, ignoring what Eddy had just said, "if the colonel says you can go on leave, you go to Winchester and you see Brigadier General Horricks. He's the only one who can authorise it. And that's why nobody applies for leave."

"Well I'm bloody well going," Eddy said.

So Eddy started off with the first written request. Then the next. And the next. He reached Colonel Fenshaw. Colonel Fenshaw's family had been in the military since the War of the Roses. George, they called him. He stuttered.

"Bloody good luck D.D.D.Dart," he said. "You d.d.deserve it. But it's very d.d.difficult."

Eddy went on to Winchester, to Regimental HQ. The regimental sergeant major interviewed him first.

"What's this?" he said. "Request to see your wife 'cos she's in the family way?"

"Yes," Eddy said. "It says so there on the note, Sergeant Major."

"You've got a bloody nerve."

"I've heard that everywhere I've been, Sergeant Major. That three parts of the invasion force's wives are in the family way. I don't give a damn if the whole invasion force is in the family way. That's nothing to do with me. That's what it says on my note."

"I see it says here you're going in any case."

"I got it laid on. I can get there, don't worry. But only for seventy-two hours."

"Brigadier General Horricks will be pleased, being pissed about by a request like this."

"Well that's regulations."

"Yes. You're quite within your rights."

Eddy marched into Brigadier General Horricks' office and gave him the snappiest salute of his army life. When he stamped to attention the inkwell shook in the desk.

Brigadier General Horricks looked up and the RSM passed Eddy's note to him. The brigadier general had big hands.

"By God," Horricks said. "Don't you think I've got anything better to do?"

"Regulations, Sir," Eddy said. "I've been and done what they tell me is regulations."

"The man's right you know, Sergeant Major. Grant it! Best of luck."

Back in the New Forest, Eddy told Colonel Fenshaw that he'd been given the leave. George was religious.

"Now look here Dart," he said. "You take a small pack as if you're going sick."

"Yes Sir," Eddy said. He would have to pass through several regiments before he reached the outskirts of the forest. Gates divided each regimental area.

"Every one of those gates you go through," George said, "you say you've gone sick. For Christ's sake don't say you're going on seventy-two hours."

Eddy reached Romsey station. On the platform were Redcaps, Canadian Redcaps, Whitecaps, Bluecaps ... They all pounced on Eddy. And at every station the train stopped, more pounced on him. And each one signed his pass. By the time he reached Torquay there was no room on it for any more signatures.

He was home for seventy-two hours. On that leave, Torquay wasn't raided.

When he got back to the New Forest the weather was scorching. One day Eddy was made Company Runner. Company Runner in the New Forest was a sod of a job: he had to mount with the guard – which meant being there for inspection at the changing of the guard – then go to the CSM, make his tea; and then run all the messages that the CSM wanted. Then, come changing of the guard in the evening, the runner had to go back to his bivouac, change into his clean uniform and mount at the back of the guard. Only then would he be dismissed. Unless he wasn't tidy enough; then he might be given evening duty.

They were living in little bivouacs they had made themselves, had to sleep on their uniforms to keep them pressed. Eddy had a bed made of boughs with turf over the top.

The officers were three miles away. The day that he was made Company Runner was particularly hot. Running through the woods, Eddy's legs were soon raw with sweat. He was knackered, chuffed off. Lunchtime, after he'd had his grub, he went for a lie down in his little bivouac.

Hoppy Hopkins woke him. "Christ, you're in the shit. The Besom down there is bloody furious."

"Why?"

"It's three o'clock. You should've been back quarter to two."

"Oh well," Eddy said. "Can't do much about it now, can he?"

Eddy went down to the Besom. The Besom could drink sixteen pints and still shoot a sixpence out of a tree. He and Eddy were alone.

"Where the fuck have you been?" he began to abuse Eddy. *He isn't allowed to call me that,* Eddy thought, *not according to regulations.*

"I'm entitled to be addressed by my rank, Sergeant Major."

"Who d'you think you're talking to?"

"And who d'you think you're talking to? I'm Gunner Dart to you, not a fucking twat."

"I'm talking to you. And count yourself lucky you're not on a charge."

"*Sans fairy anne* to me if I flop you. It's only about three days to the off. And you can't manage without me. I'm number one layer on number one gun in this bloody lot. If it wasn't for your rank, I'd bloody floor you."

"Right," Besom said. "That's it. Make the tea."

Eddy made the tea. Besom liked it strong – with so much brown sugar and condensed milk that the spoon would near stand up in the cup.

"Before you go," Besom said, "I've got to give a disciplinary talk to two officers that the Colonel's sent to me – Crawford the Biscuit and t'other one. So I'll need more tea. And you can stay and listen, see that I don't treat one rank different from the other."

The two officers came in. Eddy listened.

"You do realise," Besom said to the two officers, "that the men have to salute the King's uniform? They also salute someone inside that uniform that they respect. I don't know ... I don't know what to do with you. Especially you, Crawford. The only thing I can report to the Colonel that I can see you're any good for is to be sat on the roundabouts with a balloon on a stick ..." and so on.

When the Besom had finished with them he called Eddy back and pulled him to pieces about his uniform. Eddy had to go back to his bivouac and change.

When he returned, the Besom said: "I've got a very important message. Major Swann must have this tonight." *Oh Christ,* Eddy thought, *all the way up to the officers and back.*

"When will be the best time to go Sarge?" Eddy asked. The officers could come and go more or less as they pleased.

"Expect he's gone into Winchester," Besom said. "No telling."

On his way to find Swanny, Eddy called into the marquee. The graded down Southern Americans made lovely rock cakes. The US troops went a bundle on the rock cakes, would buy the lot. The Desert Rats were friendly only to the Desert Rats. This night the Yankees were at one long trestle table with all the rock cakes. The Desert Rats objected. A fight started. It was a madhouse – US Green Berets, US Rangers, Durham Light Infantry, British commandos – all fighting each other like in a Western.

The NAAFI girls screamed and ran out. Eddy got out through the nearest exit. The brawl brought the tent poles down. Redcaps, Canadian and Yank MPs came running. The Yank MPs had big long truncheons. As soon as they saw a lump come up in the canvas they belted it. There were almost as many casualties that night as in the Sicily invasion.

The fight was at half past ten, and Eddy had had a few pints by then. He walked up to the officers' quarters. The officers had proper tents with little shaded lights inside. Swanny wasn't in so Eddy sat across the entrance to his tent, and nodded off. Swanny wasn't a big man. Eddy woke up when Swanny tripped over him.

"Who the hell's this?" Major Swann shouted, pulling out his revolver. He then recognised Eddy. "What the hell are you doing here?" Swanny put away the revolver and went into the tent. "Come in, come in."

Eddy followed him into the light.

"Gunner Dart," Swanny said. "Why are you here two o'clock in the morning?"

"I think the invasion's started Sir."

"What the hell d'you mean?"

"Sergeant Major Leftbridge told me that you must have this message. That I must deliver it tonight. I've already been up here three times from the NAAFI. So, this time, I decided to sit here until you came."

Swanny opened the envelope, looked at the message and laughed. "What's happened between you and the Sergeant today?"

"We had a few words, Sir. He effed and blinded me, and I effed and blinded him. In fact, I threatened to put the bugger down."

"Hmmm, don't know if you could do that. He's a hard old sod. Anyhow you're excused duties. Write a note to say that – I'm a bit shaky – and I'll sign it." Major Swann had downed a few drinks himself.

When Eddy got back to his bivouac he told Hoppy to bring his breakfast up from the cookhouse in the morning, and his lunch. At lunchtime the new runner came up to Eddy. He was a Birmingham boy called Pascoe.

"The Besom wants you. Double quick. And not denims, uniform." Eddy put on his second uniform and strolled down to the Besom.

"Right! You!" Besom said to Eddy. "Two stripes. Bombardier. Backdated four months. Get up to that jewboy and get two stripes sewn on each arm. Then get back here in an hour."

"Am I going to get paid?" Eddy said. "You got too many bloody lapdogs here already. Unpaid lance corporals. I don't bloody want that."

"You'll get paid," Besom said. "I don't want any yes men as NCOs. I got no time for these unpaid stripes. And that's not a bloody favour," he added, "for getting me past that exam in Norwich. If I'd wanted I could've had you put inside for six months for speaking like that to me yesterday. So don't run away with the idea that I'm doing you any favours."

So Eddy became Bombardier Dart with backdated pay. His friends were as surprised as Eddy.

After the fight, there was no canteen. So, with nothing to do now except wait for the off, to pass the time they set up mortars in a big old quarry and gambled on shooting. Eddy won quite a bit of money – hitting the firing pin, setting them off.

A mucky little bugger called Seith used to clean out the shithouses. He came from Dumfries, was a lazy little sod. None of the men liked him. There was a notice by the incinerators telling whoever was tipping rubbish to sift through it before burning it. There was often spare ammo dumped in the rubbish. One day they heard a big bang.

A man came up to Eddy laughing. "That's Seithy gone."

"What d'you mean – gone?"

"Tired bugger, too bloody lazy to check the rubbish. He shovelled four or five hand grenades into the incinerator." It was the biggest joke of the day – no-one had liked him.

They were moved down the road to Earl Mountbatten's estate, Homelands, in Romsey. Three days before D-Day Eddy went to the cinema marquee and saw a Bing Crosby film about an Irish priest.

With time still to kill they bet pounds on heads and tails; and Eddy and all his gun crew had their heads shaved. Anything new to pass the time; even bingo and Crown and Anchor, which had been illegal in the Army before the New Forest.

Fourteen

June 4th – August 1944

June 5th 1944: Storms postpone Allied invasion of Normandy.

June 6th 1944: D-Day. Airborne divisions dropped in France. 6:00am first US seaborne troops landed. By end of the 'Longest Day', 156,000 Allied troops ashore.

June 14th-15th 1944: First USAAF bomb raids on Japan.

June 18th 1944: V1 hits Guards Chapel. Changsha taken by Japanese.

June 20th 1944: Viipuri taken by Russians.

June 21st 1944: AA guns moved from London to North Downs.

July 2nd 1944: Russians take Stolbsty.

July 3rd 1944: Russians take Minsk.

July 9th 1944: Montgomery enters Caen. RAF bombs Gelsenkirchen. Japanese in retreat from Imphal.

July 13th 1944: Russians take Vilna. AA guns massed on coast to stop V1s.

July 18th 1944: British attack over Orne gets stopped.

July 20th 1944: Attempt on Hitler's life. Allies take Saigon.

July 24th 1944: Russians take Lublin.

July 25th 1944: US troops break out of Western France ('Cobra').

July 27th 1944: Russians take Lusow, Stanislaw, Bialystok, Drinsk and Siauliai.

July 31st 1944: Patten breaks out through Avranches. Warsaw uprising as Russian troops reach outskirts.

Eddy and his crew had been training for two years for the invasion. At 2:00am on June 4th they were ordered to move. They left Romsey for Southampton, where they were halted. The streets were jammed with line upon line of armoured vehicles. And they stopped there all that day.

"Good job Jerry hasn't got an airforce now," someone said.

Women from Southampton's bombed houses brought meals out to the soldiers. Some of the men sneaked off for a quick last jump. The redcaps were riding up and down going frantic – the troops weren't supposed to speak to anybody: no-one was supposed to know that this was the invasion force.

Eddy had told Vera the date in a letter, had got past the censor by saying: 'Whatever you do don't forget Granny Gill's birthday, June 5th.' Granny Gill's birthday had been their code.

"Where d'you think they're going?" a dock woman asked a redfaced MP. "On a bloody picnic? Everybody knows where they're going. Have a drink son." And knowing where they were going, the women were prepared to do anything for the men. Eddy had ripped the backside of his trousers: he laid over the front of the gun while a woman sewed up the tear.

At 3:00pm they started to go down to their boats. By the morning of June 5th Eddy was on the same barge, with the same crew, that he had trained with in Poole and Scotland. But the sea was too rough, so all that day they waited in Southampton. Apart from the British, there were Yankee and Canadian boats. The Yanks had bottles of whiskey, handed them from boat to boat. They tried to have a sing-song. But the sea was so rough, men were being sick in the harbour.

Altogether on Eddy's barge were four self-propelled guns, a Bren carrier, and an officer's jeep up front. They had one officer for the Bren gun carrier, another with the jeep, some engineers with dynamite, and four commando Pioneers with odd-shaped bundles. No-one could figure out what the bundles were for.

At dusk that evening, the barges left harbour.

That night the Germans tried to bomb the American forces stationed in Torbay. It was a hell of a raid. But they were too late – the Yanks were already well out into the Channel.

Vera was still in the ARP and whenever she was called out, Ned would go with her to protect her with his silver-topped walking stick. She hadn't yet told the ARP that she was pregnant.

The Air Raid Warden came to the door that night. Ned answered his knock.

"What do you want?"

"Mrs Dart please. ARP. There's a raid on." The Air Raid Warden was a proper little gentleman. Trembling, Vera went to get her tin hat, her whistle and her stirrup pump.

"I can hear there's a raid on," Ned said. "What do you want?"

"They're dropping fire bombs."

"What of it?"

"Mrs Dart's in the ARP."

Ned held up his arm to Vera. "She's not coming out. She's pregnant. Goodnight." Vera was only two months gone, but Ned had spoken so that was that. As she ran to the shelter she fell against a chair.

Eddy and Hoppy Hopkins had bought a book between them. It was a long and narrow book – designed especially to fit into a battledress pocket. It was pure filth. The only other reading material they had was a letter that every soldier had been given. This was from Montgomery. He told them to forget the British idea of 'that's not cricket old boy', and that whatever the Germans did, they had to do themselves, but better.

Alongside the four guns was a channel for walking, and between that and the side of the barge, a long narrow place where the cables for dropping the ramp ran. When at sea no-one was allowed in there in case one of the cables snapped. But Eddy and Hoppy found a safe cubby-hole that had an electric light. Sitting down in there, they read to one another the juicier bits of John Smith until they fell asleep. They woke to find themselves soaking wet. The crossing was getting rougher and sea-water was coming into the barge.

At dawn they were ordered to Take Post and Strip. This order meant preparing the guns for action as fast as they could – take the covers off the barrel and the breech. Eddy could strip a breech in five seconds.

Although rough, it was a beautiful bright morning. Eddy had never seen so many ships in his life. It looked as if he could have got off his ship and walked to the next, and onto the next. If the airforce hadn't given the German coastal guns a hammering, or if the Germans had had more coastal guns, then they couldn't have missed. The Germans, though, had been deliberately led to expect the invasion at Calais.

The coast of France was in sight. The trip had taken five hours. In front of Eddy's barge were Green Howards' landing craft – Eddy's company was attached to the Green Howards. And in front of the Green Howards were the rocket ships. They fired their rockets and, their job done, they turned for home. The men who had fired the rockets all wore white asbestos suits. The rockets from just one of those ships was supposed to devastate a square half mile.

The Captain ordered Eddy's troop to commence firing. Eddy glanced to the Coventry Clock. He didn't have to use the dial sight – the clock showed him where to aim, what area to cover. They had to fire fifty rounds, reduce one hundred yards. Barge fittings flew everywhere from the concussion every time they fired the gun.

Eddy was too busy to be nervous. As layer he had to make sure that the spirit bubbles were level. With the rolling of the barge it required perfect timing. Fire fifty, reduce one hundred yards.

Their first objective was a small tower. But the infantry signalled back to the barge to tell them to stop firing on the tower because they'd knocked that out. So they went to the next target, but were almost immediately told by the infantry to stop firing because they'd knocked that out too.

Eddy was in the front of the barge. The three other guns fired over him. C troop, Charlie troop, was the senior troop in this new Commando Artillery. And Eddy's gun was number one gun of the senior troop. Major Swann was the officer in charge of Charlie troop.

Forty rounds gunfire meant that they had to get them off as fast they could. Then they had to reduce the range. Forty rounds reduce fifty. Forty rounds reduce fifty ...

They were told to load their ammo. They filled the back of the gun, loaded more onto a sled behind. They always had to have seven hundred rounds – at least – on the back. The four commando pioneers helped.

At about fifty yards from the beach they unshackled the guns. Two barges away, a landing craft of Essex Yeomanry took a direct hit. The lot went up – ammo, dynamite, and men.

Eddy noticed a lot of bodies in the water. He had expected something like this. The only thing that upset him was a steel helmet full of blood bobbing about on the surface. But he had been hardened to it: all he cared about was himself and his gun, doing what he had to do. MacDonald spewed up all over Eddy's uniform.

The Germans had erected obstacles, including mines and explosives on top of long poles placed below the high-tide mark on the beach.

But the Captain of their barge had told them: "I'll get you there. Even if I have to take you right up the bloody main road into the town."

When the barge hit the beach and the ramp went down, the first of the self-propelled guns jumped forward onto the jeep, squashing it flat. Luckily, no-one was in the jeep at the time. They eased the gun back a bit and then moved off the barge and up the beach. Their orders were to stop for nothing. The other guns followed. Meanwhile all the engineers were running off. As soon as the guns hit the sand they pulled the few bits of wire that held the waterproofing on the guns. Once they'd got rid of that they hitched up the sled with its four hundred rounds.

It had been impressed on all of them, so much so that it had become their religion, that they had to give constant cover to the infantry ahead of them. That was the reason for their existence. It meant that they had to chase hard after the infantry. If they stopped, they would leave them without cover. And the cost would be in lives.

The infantry were already about a mile and a half inland. The guns could provide cover for up to eight miles. Infantry had never had self-propelled guns before. The British had borrowed the idea from the Germans.

All that Eddy saw of the beach was the four commando pioneers. As soon as they landed, the four of them had run up the beach with their mysterious bundles, had banged them down, and up had floated four barrage balloons.

Eddy's gun was racing straight for a sunken road. German machine gun bullets whooshed over his head. The ammo sled was hooked to the back of the gun with two crossed wires. As they went up the road off the beach, the sled slewed around behind them. The sappers who had gone ahead had cleared the road of mines, but not the verges. And on every bend the sled went right up to the verge.

Their objective was to get up behind four big coastal guns and help the infantry to knock them out. Everyone knew exactly where to go because, from reconnaissance photographs, they'd built a replica of the German defences on Studley Island off Poole. And when the Germans had altered anything the mock-up had been altered. The Air Force had dropped three hundred tons of bombs on the coastal guns, but they were still working. And the bomb craters made it difficult for Eddy's gun to get close enough to fire.

They saw an opening in the concrete defences. Depressing the gun, they fired ten rounds with the caps on the shells to blast a bigger hole. Then, through that opening, they fired twenty rounds with the caps off. They could hear the shells ricocheting down the length of the hole. The infantry had already thrown hand grenades down there. Eventually the Germans surrendered, came out trembling. The hole that Eddy had fired through was in concrete thirty feet thick. The bombing the night before had only cracked it.

They pressed on, the four guns following the detachment of Green Howards. About 11:00am they stopped for a rest at a village in a valley. The infantry were on up ahead. They didn't want any firing done, so Eddy and his crew went up to a café for some coffee and cognac. They'd been given some francs and a phrasebook – "*Avez vous le beurre? Avez vous le fromage?*"

The French villagers didn't know whether to kiss them or curse them. They seemed glad that the Allies were there, but were worried that there might be a counter-attack and they would all get killed.

Apart from having his head shaved in the New Forest, Eddy had also grown a handlebar moustache, kept it greased with gun oil. To the villagers, his crew must have looked a wild lot – with their shaved heads and large moustaches. And the first women he saw in the village were all three pregnant. Eddy thought it a wonder that the women didn't drop their babies at the sight of them.

After their coffee break they did quite a bit of firing, covering the infantry in front, until they came to a crossroads called Jerusalem. Further on was the town of Tilly. They were now ten or twelve miles in from the beach.

Their first night was spent in a deep cutting below a high hedge. As soon as Eddy lay down to go to sleep he felt something crawling over him. There were small frogs everywhere. And then they started croaking, and they continued croaking throughout the night, drowning out even the noise of the guns.

They stayed on a common for two days, did a lot of firing. Mac, a brawny Highlander, hated the Germans because they'd killed his brother on the march to Dunkirk. Some of the shells were black and yellow. Mac was the loader. As he slapped the shells into the breech he would say: "Another tiger for the bastards," and then touch Eddy's shoulder as the signal to fire. Immediately after firing, Mac would shove another shell up the spout.

"Another tiger for the bastards."

They had positioned the gun next to a farmhouse on the common. The woman kept her baby in the cellar. All the soldiers sent them bars of chocolate. The farmer promised to name the baby Winston Churchill.

Colonel Fenshaw lost two of his fingers two days after D-Day. He was sent to a hospital in Bayeux where they sewed him up and gave him penicillin.

They later positioned the gun behind a high hedge on a hill above a village. The Germans were down in the valley but neither side could see the other. Charlie Troop was now on its own. Dog

Troop and the rest had gone off as sniper guns. Eddy was firing indirect fire – every evening for two hours, eighty rounds gunfire.

They were well concealed. The Germans couldn't find the gun. But one day a single German shell landed near them. The blast blew Eddy into the hedge. His back hurt a bit afterwards, but nothing much.

Colonel Fenshaw was in hospital for two days. The second day, he told his jeep driver to bring a fresh uniform and to wait for him outside the hospital that evening. Fenshaw sneaked out through a window and rejoined the regiment, going to field stations each day to get his injured hand dressed.

There were no co-ordinated battles as such in Normandy. Each group had its own little war. Eddy noticed that at times there might be a battle being fought to one side of him, while on the other side units were advancing into the countryside against no apparent resistance. But they were of no concern to Eddy – his job was to clear the road for the Green Howards.

He was amazed by the French farmers. Like everyone else, they took cover if there was an action going on close by. But, as soon as the fighting had gone half a mile past them, the farmers immediately went out into the fields to work again.

At Tilly, Eddy's gun knocked out a German light self-propelled anti-aircraft gun. This was similar to a British Bofors but mounted on its own half-track. Here they had to cover a road with a long bend in it. The Germans couldn't come down the road, the Green Howards and the Durham Light Infantry couldn't go up it.

Up ahead, two SS Tiger Tanks had dug in on a crossroad covering all the approaches. This situation held up the Green Howards' advance until the Tigers ran out of ammunition. A couple of infantrymen then knocked them out with a PIAT anti-tank weapon. Those two tank crews were the first suicide squads that Eddy had come across.

They couldn't seem to shift the Germans from Tilly, so they started firing barrages similar to those of the Great War. It was hell. They were given a programme and, no matter what the Germans were slinging back at them, they had to stick to that programme.

The sergeant was supposed to read the programme. Sergeant Ambrose was on Eddy's gun. He had been a good sergeant back in England, but here he was a bag of nerves and couldn't read the programme for stuttering.

"For fuck's sake, Sergeant," Eddy said. "Get off the bloody gun and I'll do it." So the second layer read the programme off to Eddy while Mac loaded the shells.

What they had to do was fire twenty rounds, increase the range twenty yards, fire twenty rounds, increase the range twenty yards, fire twenty rounds; and with each increase the infantry advanced twenty yards. Unfortunately the enemy 88mm guns sounded exactly the same as Eddy's twenty-five-pounder. The Germans placed their shells behind Eddy's barrage. The infantry then blamed Eddy for dropping his shells short.

Nobody liked the twenty-five-pounder shell that Eddy's gun fired. Apart from the gun crew. Like a rifle bullet, the twenty-five-pounder was made in the barrel. On any other gun, when a shell exploded in the barrel, it split like a banana and most of the crew were killed. But with a twenty-five-pounder the barrel swelled, so the gun crew at least had a chance to get away.

Once fired, however, a twenty-five-pounder shell – because it hit spinning – made an impression in dry ground only the same width as its own diameter. Where they'd been putting down barrages you couldn't get a hand's breadth between the shell holes. And the reason no-one else liked them was that when a French, German or an American shell pitched, all the shrapnel went to the side the shell had been travelling. But the twenty-five-pounder, being barrelled, the shell landed spinning and the shrapnel went all ways.

They were moved from Tilly to Falaise, back to Harcourt, then over to Caen, fighting all the time, the guns going wherever any infantry wanted them, wherever there was a push on. The ammo was brought up every night.

Behind the fighting came the first lot of Pioneers. They buried the dead. And behind that lot of Pioneers came another lot, who dug up the dead and re-buried them in proper graveyards.

Eddy's troop was re-assigned to the East Yorks. One of their officers told Eddy that they were held up at a crossroads. There were German snipers in a church tower. One officer had been killed.

Eddy's sergeant was acting as sergeant major. Daltrey was elsewhere. So Eddy found himself in charge of the gun.

"We'll come up and have a look," he said.

"No need for that," the East Yorks officer said.

"Sorry, Sir. This is my gun. And though you're an officer you're not in charge of my gun. It's no good me getting knocked out, is it?"

"I've lost five men already," the officer said.

Shouldn't have sent 'em across the bloody road, Eddy thought.

The self-propelled guns were independent units. They had their own ammo, their own supplies. If the taking of a crossroads was causing too many infantry casualties, Eddy's job was to blast hell out of the crossroads so that the infantry could safely cross. And then move forward again, following the infantry, firing where they directed him. An infantry officer could tell Eddy what he wanted done, but not how to do it. Some of them were a bit mad and would soon have got the gun knocked out. So it was up to Eddy how he did it, as long as it was done.

Mac and Eddy soon weighed up the situation. They were better at it than the officer. Moving the gun up to the right of the church, so that they were still concealed, they opened fire. Their shell knocked the top off the tower. A white flag and a big pair of white breasts appeared at the window.

"Bloody hell!" Eddy said. "Women up there. Look!" The snipers had been five SS women.

French-Canadians had got mixed up with the East Yorks. The SS women thought it would be safe to come down with their breasts showing. But as soon as they got to the bottom, the French-Canadians knifed them.

Chasing the enemy hard, with no time to spare for prisoners, they gave little boys big sticks and told them to take any prisoners back up the road to the depot. In those first weeks it was a common sight to see two boys with big sticks proudly whistling the Marsellaise as they herded their German prisoners along a road.

The Essex Yeomanry had the same type of gun as Eddy's regiment. They had landed after him. Only a week after they arrived they muddled up their map references, and the regiment went to the target area. The Germans were waiting for them.

When the Essex Yeomanry lined themselves up to fire, German Tiger tanks came out of hiding and surrounded them. All but four of their guns were captured; and those four were only saved because they were late getting there.

Each company had its own corps of Royal Electrical and Mechanical Engineers. Captain Heath was in charge of Eddy's REME. Although he was normally ten miles behind the lines, Captain Heath always fancied being in action. He wore his revolver cowboy style on his hip and his beret to one side. One day he was given the wrong map reference and, instead of going to Eddy's gun site, he went to the map reference of Eddy's target. Luckily Eddy's battery got diverted, didn't fire on that target. But that was the last they saw of Captain Heath: they assumed he must have been captured.

A Normandy farmer told Eddy that the Germans had been pretty good to them, hadn't stolen anything, and had given them enough food to keep themselves. But as soon as the Allies arrived the apples had disappeared from the trees. The Allied Command had to make stealing fruit and vegetables a court martial offence.

They came across scores of little crewcut blond boys.

"Who was your dad?"

"Bosch."

"Eyetie."

"Czech."

"Pole." None of them were ashamed of their fathers.

The Normandy women wore black stockings, looked and smelled just like big cows. Normandy itself smelled of dust and the dead.

And the peasants poured urine onto the fields from wooden barrels on carts. On a hot day the stink was awful.

Whenever possible, the gun crew dug a slit trench to sleep in at night, with one man on guard. Other crews sat guard on the gun. But Eddy decided against that because some Germans had crept up and had lobbed a grenade into an open gun. With a slit trench they could at least cover it.

And as soon as they got into the slit trench – dead tired – and lay down to sleep, the small frogs began crawling all over them. The men kept their helmets on when they slept, but with the strap off – so that if any shrapnel got into the helmet it would lift it off rather than ricochet inside it.

At night there were enough glow-worms in the hedgerows to write a letter by.

Eddy was now the only layer on his gun. Drainpipe, the trainee doctor, although he'd been a good layer in England, had lost his nerve soon after landing. He had been assigned to HQ. Sergeant Ambrose could lay the gun, but he was more interested in being a sergeant major. Mac, though, was level-headed, always on the look-out, never missed much – and he was a good shot too.

One officer was an architect's assistant from London. The men were all given Benzedrine to keep them going. But this officer kept on taking it. One day he crouched down so far in the trench that he couldn't hear the firing orders – he was lying over the radio set. Sergeant Eyelett, a Cockney, went over and threatened to shoot him if he didn't get up. The next day the officer took off like a sprinter for the German lines, and was never seen again.

One day, near Tilly, the infantry was under heavy fire from German mortars. Major Swann was unable to range the guns on them. So he sneaked right up to the German mortars, radioed back his position and gave the order to fire. His guns blew the German mortars to pieces and Major Swann with them.

Major Swann's jeep driver – a quiet man, who never drank or smoked – went in to fetch him, got his arm shattered doing it. But they couldn't do anything for Swanny, couldn't even touch him, he was in so much pain. He died and was awarded the Military Cross posthumously. Eddy felt he should have got the Victoria Cross.

Not until three weeks after D-Day did they meet any real Germans. The German troops they had met up until then had all been Czechs, Poles or Rumanians.

The first SS men Eddy captured didn't give a damn.

"So you may have got to Bayeux," they told him. "We are in Birmingham in England. We have captured London, advanced on Southampton. Before you get out of Normandy we will have captured all of England."

The SS may have believed it, but Eddy didn't. The SS had also been told that the Allies would torture and kill all their prisoners. One of the first lot of German prisoners Eddy took, he put to dig ammunition pits. The Germans were convinced they were digging their own graves.

Normandy was flat, with orchards and high hedges along the lanes. The worst possible terrain to fight over. If they got caught in an orchard the shrapnel would just rain down off the apple trees. The Germans got very good at airbursts, could make them burst at six feet or at any height they chose. Same with mortars.

The airbursts killed cows. Some fields were full of dead cows. And they stank. The men had bets on maggot jumping. Injured cows were walking about with lumps of shrapnel in them. And those cows not wounded had milk fever from not being milked. Those soldiers who had worked on farms milked them.

One day Eddy's crew found a stray cow. They tied it up to a tree. That night a shell burst by the tree and in the morning all that was left to mark the spot was the piece of rope that had tethered the cow.

Another day they came upon a wounded cow. A soldier reckoned he was a butcher. He killed it, cut out the liver and they had it fried. The following day Eddy and his crew suffered diarrhoea attacks – over the side of the gun, in the gun, in their pants, in action. The liver had been too fresh.

Luckily they all survived. If the authorities had found out they'd eaten a cow they'd all have been court martialled. They were not supposed to eat anything other than their own rations, not even drink water they didn't carry with them. The Germans had poisoned the wells. So the British troops used the wells to have baths over. They'd soap themselves, hook a rope under their arms, and lower themselves into the well for a rinse. The water was freezing.

At night, black Americans brought the ammunition up to the gun. They hated the dark, but didn't mind bringing up British ammo because they could tip it, something they didn't dare attempt with US shells which were too sensitive.

In one place Eddy's gun had high poplar trees behind it. The German shells were whistling through the top of the poplars when the ammunition trucks arrived. In the dark, all that the gun crew could see of the drivers was the whites of their eyes rolling worriedly as the enemy shells ripped through the treetops.

"Yeah man. Let's get this ammo off."

"You're supposed to stack it," they were told. Eddy and the crew liked to kid them.

"We ain't stacking it, man."

"The bloody lot could go up tipping it like that."

"You want to get the hell out of here," Carrington chipped in. "We had a counter-attack last night just after you'd gone."

They tipped the ammo. And they were amazing drivers, could follow a chalk line in the dark, all of them on a hill changing gear at exactly the same spot.

One day the crew had no potatoes with their rations, so that night they went foraging. As they worked their way along a row of potatoes in a field, they noticed figures working their way towards them along the next row. They were Germans. They passed each other by without a word.

In Charlie troop they had an officer whose father owned a chain of garages around Watford. He was a good looking man with curly hair. One day his gun was going along a narrow lane. With the high hedges the gun had no room to turn around. The Germans mortared both ends of the lane. It was a common tactic. A piece of shrapnel took off the soft part of the officer's nose. After that he lost his nerve, was no good. Doolally-tap.

Eddy admired the infantry. The Lancaster bombers would come over, knock out the main resistance, then go home to England. The infantry then had to go in and clear up what was left. And the infantry had to stay there, could only occasionally get to the rear for a pint of beer and a game of football. And it was usually the county regiments of infantry that got the dirtiest jobs. The Guards would be given the glory of a big attack; but a county regiment would then have to hold it against any counter-attack, which very often was a bloody sight worse.

Mac was an exceptionally kind man. Except to the Germans. Eddy had to keep an eye on him or he would have shot all the prisoners they took, wounded as well. One day, three Germans who had surrendered laughed nervously at Mac's accent. Mac's throaty, "Raus!" was similar to theirs. Mac shot all three of them.

They had one officer, Mr Daltrey, whose father's estate was next to Baldwin's. Braces they called him. He was six feet tall and extremely thin.

Braces would come up to the guns, say to Eddy: "We'll put their little tails up Bombardier." And Eddy would think, *Oh Christ I wish he'd shift from here.*

Back in England Eddy had been on an OPAck course. It had been a cushy number – going up to the command post, siting the guns and bringing them up to target. In England there'd been two of them on their own up on the moors drawing panoramas all day. But Normandy was such close country, instead of sitting on a hill at the command post behind the lines, they had to go up ahead of the infantry. OPAcks were getting killed ten a penny.

One week into the Normandy campaign, Braces took over OPAck and took Eddy with him. Their carrier driver, Clarky, came from Bridgwater.

"Christ," he said to Eddy. "You've jumped in the shit now." He drove them to a farmhouse on a hill.

"This looks pretty good," Braces said. Eddy groaned inwardly, knowing that the Germans would soon figure out where they were spotting from. But he went up to the farmhouse with Braces. Bernard from Nottingham and Pete Hornet followed. Pete Hornet was an OPAck too. Bernard drove the half-track.

Down below the farmhouse were seven or eight hundred Germans. They were having a rest. The cook wagons were there, they were mending their socks, scrubbing up, shaving.

Braces chuckled. "Oh won't we put their little tails up."

Montgomery had a new stunt, which avoided putting a range shell down. Now they could bring all their guns to bear at the same time. Stonking it was called. So all three batteries and heavy machine guns would hit them at the same time – the big guns firing first so as to arrive on target all at once.

Eddy had never seen anything like it. One moment the German troops were all sitting about relaxing, the next the shells burst among them. And the guns kept the barrage going, knocked hell out of them.

"I thought we'd put their little tails up Bombardier," Braces said.

"I'm fucking off out of this," Pete Hornet said. "Down the cellar."

A little while later – phewitt! The top of the farmhouse roof came off, the chimney collapsed and all the ceilings came down.

"Hah," Braces said. "Thought they'd find us. Bound to unless they were bloody stupid. Anyhow, I've got enough time to put some more over there. You chaps don't want to stay here though. You go back down to the bottom."

"Right," Eddy said. "We will."

They went, and waited. Braces came down later covered in plaster.

The men liked Braces.

It was cold now at night, driving rain during the day. Although there were only five in Eddy's crew, they had rations sent up for eight. At night they made their bivouac beside the gun.

"Oxo?" Braces would shout over from his trench. The gunners had the stock cubes sent out from home and used them to make hot beef drinks.

"Yes Sir. Come on." And Braces would crawl over to them.

Besom didn't come up the line. It was his job as Battery Sergeant Major to organise the ammunition. By rights Besom had been too old for active service, and though he may have been a poor scholar, he was a good organiser. One day he came up to the front on his motorbike. He carried two revolvers. When he reached Eddy's gun he said: "I shot a German back there in the hedge. Sniper I think."

Pete Hornet, who was driving the officer's half-track, was there. "Where was that, Sergeant Major?" he asked.

"Back along," Besom said.

"That bugger's been dead in that hedge for about five weeks."

"Never."

"Yeah."

"Well I never seen him there before. He looks exactly like a sniper. He's got a rifle. Nobody's picked it up."

"He's been there at least five weeks to my knowledge," Pete Hornet said.

"Well I've made sure he's dead now, am't I? I had to shoot some bugger somewhere."

They were told to be on guard against everyone. There were some English-speaking Germans in British uniforms with British guns operating behind the British lines. A lot of British got killed by their own men because of them.

The British troops only had little waterproof capes. They were no use at all on the gun. And it rained. And it was hot. The valley of the Orne was swarming with mosquitoes. Little Switzerland that was called. Eddy found a German officer's coat, a long one. It kept him dry until a British soldier saw him from a distance and took a shot at him. After that Eddy stuck to the cape.

By this time none of the infantry was walking. They had German staff cars, horses and carts, bicycles – anything they could lay their hands on. When they advanced now, there was very little show of discipline. It was like a rabble.

Many of the troops had picked up German weapons. Eddy had got hold of a Visa. It made a be-be-be-be-be noise when fired. The

British equivalent went da-da-da-da-da. No-one knew who was firing at who. The order came through to stop using them.

Behind the infantry came the self-propelled guns, behind the guns the ambulances. Eddy didn't envy the stretcher bearers their job. He saw the Yorks fighting, and they lost a lot of men. He saw the Pioneer Corps burying the dead. And he saw them break the arms and legs of the corpses with pickaxe handles so that they could get them into the graves. One load of dead was bundled into blankets. The padre said a few words over them as they were dropped into a pit. The bodies were all blue.

When the Germans attacked it was with a crack division in front, followed by the Wehrmacht, followed by the SS – to stop the Wehrmacht retreating. Many German troops attempting to retreat were shot by the SS. But as soon as the Wehrmacht got rid of the SS, they surrendered in droves. Eddy often passed fifty or so with their rifles stacked by the roadside waiting to surrender.

One day Eddy and Mac's guns were sent up onto a plain, and took up position on a long corner. They had no idea what they were supposed to be doing, but they had been told to stay there and keep an eye out for anything on the plain up ahead. They took a walk out in front of their guns. Something was coming towards them. Eddy took out a pair of field glasses.

He said to Mac: "What the bloody hell's this? There's a bloody battleship coming up the road."

All that Eddy could see above the hedges was a huge naval gun. It was a Leopold. The Germans had used them in Russia. Mac and Eddy ran back to their self-propelled guns and loaded up Armour Piercing shells. AP shells had extra packing of cordite, but against German tanks and guns they were only effective at seven hundred yards' range. They aimed both guns at the approaching Leopold.

They couldn't afford to miss. As the Leopold came around the corner they fired, hit it, and knocked it out. They walked over to have a look. The German gun crew had all been killed. Just then the Germans started shelling the road, and so they were sent back.

Having been told to stay on the plain that evening they went down among some trees. There were a few infantry down there asleep with a lot of German prisoners inside a square of rope.

That night Eddy didn't bother digging a trench. He sat on guard inside the gun. The younger men couldn't stay awake, and when there was anything happening Eddy couldn't sleep. He could go for days without sleep, so more often than not he stood guard.

Sitting down hidden inside the gun, with the Sten cradled in his arms to cover both sides, he lit a cigarette. A silhouette appeared suddenly from nowhere. It was a German.

"Don't fire, boyo," a voice called out. "Don't fire."

I'm bloody dreaming, Eddy thought, *a Welshman in German uniform?* Keeping him covered, Eddy climbed off the gun.

"You're bloody lucky I didn't blow your head off. What's your game?"

The Welshman explained.

Before the war he had married a German girl, had taken German citizenship. She had died. He had returned to Cardiff. According to him, the German authorities had traced him there and had conscripted him back to Germany – he hadn't bothered reverting to British citizenship. He had been forty-five years old at the time and the Germans had put him in their Pioneers. He had walked such a distance to reach the allied lines that blood was oozing from his boots.

"You're still bloody lucky I didn't blow your head off, Taff," Eddy said.

"I wish I'd been impounded. Anything but this."

"Ah well, come with me," Eddy said.

He nudged Mac to tell him where he was going, and he took Taffy down to where the other prisoners were being held. About three hundred of them were roped off. About twenty British soldiers snored outside the rope. The Germans snored inside.

"Get yourself in there," Eddy told him. And unseen by either the British or the Germans, Taff crawled under the rope and lay down on the ground.

Taff stayed with Eddy's crew for a while, washed all their clothes for them. One day Army Intelligence arrived and took him away for questioning.

Vera was five months' pregnant. The RAF was chasing some Focke-Wolfes back from Plymouth. The Focke-Wolfes jettisoned their bombs over Torquay. Vera and her mother went running to the shelter. Vera tripped and fell on her stomach. She received a few bruises but was otherwise alright.

Ned helped Vera into the shelter where he gave her some brandy.

"Have some more, Maid," he told her. Vera's mother was so frightened that she had fouled herself.

"Have some more, Maid," Ned told Vera again. Vera was so drunk, so warm and comfortable, she couldn't have cared less if the world had ended.

Eddy was in the gun going along a narrow road back up to the line for an attack. He was dirty with smoke and oil. A man coming the other way, driving a water cart, was just as dirty. They had just enough room to pass. As they drew alongside, the man on the water cart shouted out, "Ellacombe for Ellacombe!"

"Ellacombe for Ellacombe!" Eddy shouted back; and had just enough time to recognise Frank Endicott. Then they were past one another.

The first man Eddy had seen in Normandy that he knew and he hadn't been able to stop for a chat. And he puzzled on it all the way back up to the line: Frank Endicott was supposed to be in the Engineers blowing up bridges, not driving a water cart.

For two months the Allies had been trying to break out of Normandy. Unable to break through at Caen, and having plenty of artillery already there, Eddy's troop was sent up to a big plain near Hottot.

The Duke of Wellington's was on one side of a road, the King's Own Scottish Borderers on the other. Both were infantry. The Duke of Wellington's had heard a rumour that six Tiger tanks and some German self-propelled guns were coming up, so they had retreated, leaving the KSBs up there on their own. The Duke of Wellington's were still going back as Eddy and his troop moved forward.

Once there, grumbling about the Duke of Wellington's, and not looking forward to tangling with six Tiger tanks, they found themselves good positions. A Tiger tank appeared. All four guns of Charlie troop hit it. If the Tiger had seen them first he would more than likely have put all four of them out. The Tiger's 88 was deadly – effective up to two thousand yards.

The Duke of Wellington's and the KSBs then advanced. Eddy and the three other guns covered them. And all along the road with its poplar trees were loads more British artillery, mostly 45s. The Germans brought up more Tiger tanks and repulsed the advance.

They were on the Hottot plain for some time. They tried a new tactic. At night they trained searchlights on the German lines and fired from behind the lights. One night as they started firing they saw British planes overhead, coming back from a bombing run. The planes had their green lights on. But among the British planes were some German planes copying the green recognition lights on the wingtips.

The German aircraft attacked the guns on the plain. Four of the 45s were knocked out, and two of the self-propelled guns went up. And the searchlights were still on, so the Germans came down and destroyed them too.

From there, Eddy's gun was sent to St Lo to help the Americans. The American 105s were no good as howitzers, whereas the British self-propelled guns, if they took out the 202 charge and fired only charge 2, could fire almost vertically, lobbing shells over the hills. And there were hills all around St Lo. It was a piece of cake.

They set the gun up in a beautiful orchard, the hill before them, and only had to fire twice a day. Nearby was a village called Ballycouen, and further on down the valley was Couer de Seur, another big village with plenty of cafés. Leaving two men on the gun, they could stroll down to the villages for a drink, buy butter and eggs. There were hundreds of dogs roaming about. They never saw the Yanks, although they were there, in the hills around them.

They were then sent to Caumont. There was a German 88 about five miles from them. He would fire so many rounds and then stop. Eddy's job was to fire two hundred rounds in reply – one every six minutes on a fixed dial and range. They all had a go, but still the German 88 kept firing – so many rounds, then stop.

Eddy and the rest kept firing at this 88 and couldn't understand why they hadn't hit it. For two weeks they fired their two hundred rounds daily, and the German 88 fired its few, then stopped. During this time, allied forces built up behind the guns ready for a push.

Instead of going through Caen, the Generals had decided to make the break through Caumont. Seven o'clock one morning they were told that one thousand low flying Lancasters were going to drop their bombs two hundred and fifty yards in front of the guns. Dead on time they came. The bombs fell out of the sky, and not one landed closer than two hundred and fifty yards from the guns.

When the bombing started, the guns were loaded up ready for the big push. They were having a cup of tea – brewed on a tin of petrol in the gun. They couldn't drink it for shaking. And as soon as the bombing stopped they made their dash five miles forward.

All was black and smoking. Germans emerged from holes in the ground calling '*Kamarade*', blood coming from their ears. But, once they had advanced the five miles, it was as if the bombing had never taken place. The Germans were dug in as tight as before.

However, they did discover why they had been unable to knock out the German 88. It was on rails in a long tunnel. Out it had come, banged off ten rounds, then they had rolled it back into the safety of the tunnel.

The village houses had cob walls. In some villages the Germans had reinforced those walls with two feet of concrete. Eddy watched the Somerset Light Infantry attack one of these fortified villages.

It was held by the German Death's Head Hussars. Eddy had done the shelling, and moved in when the village was taken. He saw then what a battle there had been to take the school. The Germans there had fought to the last man. The children's paintings and books were scattered everywhere, over dead British and German soldiers.

They were out of petrol for three days. The gun held six hundred and fifty gallons, and they normally refuelled at night. But armed gangs of American and British deserters had stopped the convoy on its way to the line and hijacked all the petrol. From what Eddy heard, there were about ten thousand American and seven thousand British deserters. Every five weeks, everyone, except those who were fighting, were confined to barracks so that the Military Police could round up the deserters.

Eddy and the crew weren't too bothered by the lack of petrol. They had run out next to a café, and so sat there drinking *café au lait.* They would have been quite happy if fresh petrol had never appeared.

Unfortunately for them it did, and one night a little later, with nobody knowing where they were, except that it was near Evrercy, they rolled up outside the entrance to a large house. Gilbert Carrington, the driver, was very windy. This night he wouldn't come out of the slit trench to help on the gun. Eddy wanted the gun moved.

"If you don't come out of that pissing trench," Eddy said, putting the Sten to Gilbert's ear, "I'll blow your fuckin' head off."

"Don't do that, Bombardier."

Later Gilbert asked Eddy: "You meant that, didn't you?"

" 'Course I bloody meant it," Eddy said. "If we hadn't moved then, three other blokes could've copped it as well as you."

Gilbert Carrington was an excellent driver though. He kept the gun repaired with bits of wire; and nobody could get away quicker than him. He also had other uses. If they were in a big town he would go out and pick the pockets of the Yanks. So they were never short of anything.

On July 18th the British tank attack over the Orne was stopped. Eddy had joined the Wessex division for that one. The fighting had been all over the place – up hills and down dales. Although it had been fairly easy for Eddy – they'd been on top of the hills firing down.

After that they started to break out. Young Jock, recovered from his mumps, rejoined them. They got through the valley of the Orne, and after Caumont they were at Ilpican – again with the 33rd Wessex.

The Ilpican valley was bombed heavily and Eddy had a terrific backache. During a lull in the fighting he went down to a First Aid centre at a crossroads. Taking his rifle, he crept down beside a hedge. There were bomb craters everywhere. A little sign was poking up over the top of one of them. His own doctor was in there.

He was a big man, from the 8th Army. Eddy liked him.

"Hello Bombardier," the doctor said. "What do you want?"

"I've come about my backache."

"I'll have a look at you in a minute. It's a bit quiet."

No sooner had he said that than the Germans started shelling again and for about half an hour it was pretty rough. A man with a lump of shrapnel hanging out of his neck was brought in. And while Eddy had been gone from Charlie troop, the Germans had hit one of the guns. Some Tiger tanks were dug in up ahead.

The sergeant on the gun was brought in with a hole in his guts. The shell had gone into the gun and bounced around inside it, before going in Sergeant Johnstone's guts and out through his shoulder blades. He was an oldish sergeant for their regiment – thirty-eight. The doctor and a medical orderly asked Eddy to give them a hand.

The man with the shrapnel in his neck turned out to be nothing serious – a long thin piece of metal had penetrated just under the skin. The doctor pulled it out.

"What a bloody fuss, man. Get off with you." For Johnstone they put five shell dressings in the hole in his stomach. Johnstone, a Londoner, smoked while they were doing this. He was normally very cheerful.

"What chance I got?" he asked the doctor.

"Well ... let's throw away that bit." Eddy didn't see what the doctor took out and threw away. "You'll not want that anymore. Now you've got a fifty-fifty chance."

Eddy left without receiving attention to his back. It had seemed a pathetic complaint compared to the others. He found out later that Johnstone survived.

The Duke of Cornwall's infantry was at Ilpican. Eddy's gun covered their attack on a hill. The Duke of Cornwall's went up that hill three times, each time taking high casualties. What was left of them took the hill on the third attempt.

They had broken out of Normandy.

Fifteen

August – October 28th 1944

August 1st 1944: Polish underground massacred.

August 8th 1944: Japanese take Hengyary.

August 10th 1944: Pacific Allies win Battle of Aitape. British regaining ground in Burma.

August 23rd 1944: Rumanians go over to Russia.

August 25th 1944: Paris taken by Allies.

August 27th 1944: Russians take Galatz.

August 29th 1944: 2nd Army dashes from Seine to Antwerp, over-runs V1 sites. RAF bombs Konigsberg. Saipan taken by Allies.

August 30th 1944: Russians take Ploesti oilfields.

August 31st 1944: Patten's 3rd Army crosses Meuse at Verdun, then runs out of petrol. Russians take Bucharest. Georg Elser executed.

September 3rd 1944: British 2nd Army enters Brussels.

September 4th 1944: 11th Armoured Division captures Antwerp. Germany's 'First Parachute Army' on the Albert Canal.

September 8th 1944: V2s begin. Russia declares war on Bulgaria. Bulgaria declares war on Germany. Russia occupies Bulgaria.

September 15th 1944: Finns declare war on Germany. Allies held up at Aachen.

September 17th 1944: 'Blackout' ends. 'Dimout' allowed.

September 18th 1944: Arnhem massacre.

September 19th 1944: Allies take Brest. Russians take Temesoara.

September 22nd 1944: Russians take Arad.

October 1944: Allies win Battle of Leyte Gulf.

October 11th 1944: Russians take Cluj and Memel.

October 13th 1944: Russians take Riga.

Eddy made the breakout with the 11th Armoured Division. Then, while the rest of his regiment's guns were being used conventionally, D troop and Charlie troop were designated sniper guns. For four weeks they helped the French Resistance bang out a few Germans.

The French Resistance were living in a cave. Most of them were bandits or Spaniards, and – so far as Eddy could see – were out to feather their own nests. Only a few were genuine. Carrington found a hoard of rings that the Resistance had taken off German prisoners. Then he found the prisoners' bodies – the Resistance had thrown petrol over them and burned them. Eddy told Carrington to keep quiet about it.

Eddy came across his first Gestapo corpses. They were green. He was told that they went that odd colour because of the drugs they had been taking.

They picked up a rabbit at a farmhouse. It had long floppy ears. They Christened him Wilfred and kept him in an ammunition case inside the gun. When they stopped, they let him out to feed. He didn't take much notice when they fired, but if they were on the receiving end he hopped quickly back to the gun. They soon learned to watch him. Wilfred seemed to know in advance that something was afoot.

Back with the 11th Armoured they chased after the retreating Germans. They raced through village after village in hot pursuit, the French shouting at them, pointing the way: "*Allemagne – huit!*"

Neither side was supposed to loot. But the Germans looted the British dead, and the British did the same with German corpses. The last thing the Germans threw away when they were retreating was their loot.

During an advance they would first find a big stack of rifles that the Germans had thrown away. And then, further on, loads of loot. They would then stop the gun and pick up the watches and the rings. At one stage Eddy was in possession of approximately four thousand rings. He strung them up under the gun.

Before the Allies had finished taking Amiens, the Resistance were out rounding up the collaborators. Eddy saw them hang one man from a lamp-post. They stood him on top of a van, put the rope around his neck, started the van and left him hanging.

Before he left Amiens Eddy saw three more men hanging from lamp-posts. The Resistance shaved the heads of women collaborators and paraded them on carts. So far as Eddy could see it was all a convenient means of settling old scores.

For the poor girls it was simply propaganda – many of those doing the shaving had been black-marketeers who had dealt with the Germans. The British troops didn't like the French mobs, and shouted out as they passed: "Leave 'em alone, you Froggie bastards."

Their leap of the leapfrog was over. They had cleared the way. Now it was time to sit back and watch others do the push. Their turn would come again. They rested up at a chateau called Chantilly. It had racing stables and a little racecourse. Those who could ride raced the horses. The rest placed bets.

There was also a large pond with dragonflies bigger than any Eddy had ever seen in England. Eddy made himself a line, did some fishing. Others fished with hand grenades.

Gilbert Carrington used a rope to move dead Germans, in case they were booby-trapped. Eddy couldn't bring himself to touch the dead. He bartered for his rings.

In one town they came to there was no-one but Eddy, the four crew on the gun and a few stray dogs. So they went into the two jewellery stores and helped themselves. Looting was a court martial offence; but the officers did it as well.

Relieving Germans of their loot, Eddy came by several British watches that the Germans had taken off British dead. By way of a German he got a beautiful watch from a Sherwood Forester.

They were moving through one village, hard on the heels of the Germans, when the villagers came running out.

"*Allemagne! Allemagne!* That way! Taken all!" And the villagers came chasing after the gun. The first German they caught up with was not only loaded down with framed pictures and a bundle of clothes, but he had two brand new piano accordions strapped to him as well. He had thrown his gun away.

It was difficult getting money for the loot. Some Germans they captured had money, so they bartered with them. Then they heard that there was one place where they could buy postal orders to send home. They couldn't get back there to buy them themselves, so they tried giving the money to supply troops to buy them on their behalf. But that was the last they saw of the money; although they assumed the families of the supply troops received a stack of postal orders.

There was no cover on the gun. If it rained, the men were all soon soaked through and the walkways became slippery. So they found some old iron stays, bent them, wired them into the corners of the gun and stretched a tarpaulin over the top. At that time they had a hen coop with three hens on the back of the gun – for a supply of eggs. Others guns had dogs. With the hens, the tarpaulin, and the German rifles they collected to hand over to the Resistance, the self-propelled gun was like a travelling circus.

An order came through to scrap the lot. They got rid of the tarpaulin, the hens and the rifles, but kept Wilfred the rabbit.

The objective of the 11th Armoured was to get to Antwerp as fast as possible. They raced through towns that had been bombed flat. Not bothering with opposition to their sides, they just knocked out anything that was directly in front, and pressed on. Those bringing up the rear dealt with any enemies that they left.

They arrived in Boom, a brick-making town, accompanied by the Middlesex Regiment's heavy machine guns. Eddy's gun pulled into a long boulevard with trees. It had German slit trenches and machine gun posts along its entire length. But not one of them was manned. The Germans had not expected the Allies to reach there so fast.

There was a large barracks in Boom. The commander of the barracks refused to surrender. His troops, however, did; and they brought their commander out with them. The barracks stores were packed with whisky. On leaving there, every gun had about five crates of whisky on the back and most of the infantry were three parts cut.

At Antwerp the Germans were using V1 rockets as artillery. As fighting progressed in the city, Eddy could see the V1s taking off – a mass of bright lights, and in the vapours behind the rocket, a rainbow. Many of them appeared to turn around and go back.

Eddy positioned his gun in a small park. By now the gun was so worn out that the recoil didn't work properly. Recoil oil was expensive stuff – most of the gunners used it on their hair. Now every time they fired they had to push the gun back. Eddy was certain that sooner or later the gun was going to blow up and that would be the end of them.

When they finished firing they were sent back ten miles to their REME depot, and stayed there for eight hours. Apart from damaged guns there were tanks and aeroplanes there. Eddy and the crew took a look around, saw Pioneers use steam hoses to wash out what was left of some the tank crews before repairing the tanks. Their own guns that had been knocked out had been replaced and manned by Czechs to bring their regiment up to strength.

The engineers dismantled his old gun, lifted it out with a crane, dropped in a new one and lined it up. But the whole vehicle had pretty near had it. It was only doing one mile to the gallon, and the bogey wheels were worn out.

They went back into Antwerp, fought all the way through it. Two German submarines were in dry dock. Their deck guns were holding up the infantry. Eddy's gun bulldozed into a warehouse. The warehouse had large shutter windows. From there they fired at the submarines and hit both of them, knocking out their guns.

More Germans were across the river. Eddy's gun went into the grounds of a luxury hotel. The infantry were inside the hotel, with all the windows sandbagged up. It only needed a couple of soldiers on watch. So the rest lazed about in there, slept between silk sheets and washed under gold taps.

Their orders were to open fire on any Germans they saw across the river. One German appeared on a pushbike. Everyone opened up and the German disappeared in an explosion of dust. It was a waste of ammunition, the sort of thing they accused the Yanks of doing. The order soon came through for them to stop it.

One afternoon a V1 landed on a cinema full of troops, killing three thousand.

After Antwerp, Eddy's battery was made part of a smaller unit and was sent off to do some stonking – working behind the German lines. As well as the four self-propelled guns there were some Nottingham tanks, five Sherwood Forester tanks, three armoured cars, three truckloads of infantry, and some anti-tank guns.

They crossed at night further down the Albert Canal from where the fighting was, drove fifty miles further into Belgium, until they came to some woods in the morning. When the Belgians saw them they nearly swallowed their tongues. They were told to say nothing.

The guns, tanks and infantry sat in the woods and waited. The woods overlooked a railway line. At about eleven o'clock a German troop train came along. The guns opened up, killed the lot.

The officer in charge of the stonking was in the Sherwood Foresters. He was a ginger man, public schoolboy type, flying handlebar moustaches and no sympathy. He killed Germans for no reason.

"Wipe them all out. Finish. General Montgomery said in his letter: 'No kid gloves.' Wipe them all out. No more trouble."

A favourite trick of the Sherman tank crews was to approach German slit trenches, put the tank into a slide and fill in the slit trench, burying alive whoever had been in it. The German tanks did it too. 'No kid gloves'.

The train, though, had been full of young boys from the Luftwaffe who had been seconded to the front. Their rifles had still been packed in grease. Those few that survived were taken prisoner and a couple of armoured cars marched them to Antwerp.

Eddy went for a walk around a burnt out copse. He found three German boys in there, about seventeen years old. They had a big hamper full of German pork. Eddy took them back to his gun. They all had a good feed.

And there they waited for three days for the bulk of the advancing forces to catch up with them.

Because of rationing, Vera was worried that she wasn't getting the proper food for the baby she was carrying. Vera Toms occasionally came to the rescue. She'd ring Maison Vee's.

"Hello," the jaw would crack. "This is your friend speaking. We're frying tonight. Come down at eight o'clock. The lot of you." So at eight o'clock all the girls from the shop would go down to the Epicure, where Vera Toms always saved Vera a steak.

Eddy's troop was one of the first to arrive at the Hescott Canal on the Dutch border. He kept up a steady fire while the rest built up behind them.

At first, leaving a couple of men on the gun, they'd taken turns to nip back a couple of miles for a drink. Then the Germans started sending suicide tanks through – a few SS on Tigers. The Allied lines let them pass, and then they were blown up. Army Intelligence, though, kept telling them that the Germans had no tanks left in Holland.

It was here that Eddy first saw jet aircraft in action – Germans. They dropped anti-personnel bombs – single six foot steel canisters packed with very thin anti-personnel shrapnel, the kind of stuff that took arms and legs clean off. Eddy couldn't understand why they didn't hit C troop's four guns; because they were sited in an open field beside a road and the Germans bombed the road several times, killed the regiment's captain quartermaster – a fat little chap. Eddy saw the bomb score a direct hit on the jeep.

All along the Hescott Canal, which ran the length of the Belgian/Dutch border, was the Hermann Goerring Division. It was made up of young SS, boys of only fourteen or fifteen, like the Boys' Brigade for schoolboys back at home. And they wouldn't give in, were the worst that Eddy had come up against. They had been indoctrinated from birth: Hitler was their god.

German propaganda announced that the Allies were killing children. They were. But these children had weapons. Those they captured were odd – men/boys. They told of the women they'd had – little hardcases; and they were only fourteen years old.

Events had now become oddly routine. For instance, when the infantry and the self-propelled guns arrived at the Hescott Canal, the guns dug in and kept banging away, while they waited for the big build-up behind them. This build-up, prior to another big push forward, went on for some time.

As Eddy's was a crack regiment, he was to be assigned to the Guards for the coming advance into Holland. Before the Guards would accept them, however, they sent someone down to see what the gunners drilled like. A squad of gunners, with rifles, marched up and down, in and out. The gunners were as good as the Guards; and none of them was offended at having to drill – while they were drilling they weren't fighting.

It was there, in the cold, that the King paid them a visit. They all had to clean up a bit, although the British were fussy about keeping clean anyway. Where amongst the US or Germans the troops shit anywhere, the British would be court martialled if they didn't take a shovel, dig a pit and bury it. Eddy only caught a glimpse of the King as he passed along the ranks, but afterwards they all agreed that the man looked nearly dead.

Where they were on the canal, there was only one road into Holland. And only one bridge over the canal – a small humpbacked bridge no wider than one on a country road over a small river. Twenty-two-thousand vehicles an hour had to cross this tiny canal bridge; and then advance sixty-four more miles – all along a narrow road, against German opposition – in three days. The objective, besides invading Holland, was to capture the Arnhem Bridge over the Rhine. They were told that thousands of American paratroops were going to be dropped on the towns of Eindhoven and Nijmegen, along with a British airborne division at

Arnhem. They all had orders to capture and hold their respective bridges until relieved. This concerted attack was supposed to end the war before Christmas. They'd heard that before.

Army Intelligence still maintained that the Germans had no tanks in Holland. So Eddy's battery set off across the bridge behind the Guards Armoured. In the first nine miles the Guards lost twenty tanks – shot up by Tiger tanks.

Despite that, they reached a little place outside Eindhoven before daylight. Eddy sited his gun in one garden, another in another garden – so that they covered the approaches to the village. The Dutch people poked little Union Jacks up through holes in their roofs. When the German counter attack came, they pulled them quickly back. When the counter attack was driven off, up came the Union Jacks again. Beer was then passed out to the troops, schnapps handed around. A few German shells came over. The beer and the Dutch villagers disappeared.

The guns were then ordered to advance into Eindhoven, a town about the size of Bristol. The Germans bombed Eindhoven as Eddy went through it. The men worried about all the ammunition stacked on the back of the vehicle and the petrol below it. The faster they went the happier they were.

Eddy's troop was ordered to the other side of Eindhoven to support US Airborne troops. When they first arrived, the Yanks thought that C troop's guns were peashooters. Eddy told Mac not to say anything. "Wait till they get the blast."

The guns were positioned in a staggered line as usual. The 25s had a terrific recoil on them. The Yanks had dug in beside the guns where, firing at that angle, they would get the blast. Eddy's ears had bled the couple of times he had been caught on the wrong side of the guns. Normally they wore earplugs on a piece of string. The guns also recoiled five feet on their tracks. They began firing. The Yanks moved.

One of the Yanks had been a gangster – had been in prison for murdering his mother, talked Bronx. He was a liar, came back one day with a sword, said he'd captured a German Field Marshall.

"Where's the Field Marshall, then?" Eddy asked him.

"Shot him, boy. Didn't I?"

Once C troop started firing they couldn't go wrong with the Yanks. American Majors came down to congratulate them. They were given English rations, Yank rations – the Yanks had never seen artillery like it. The British system was far quicker and more accurate than the Yanks'. The British didn't do any range firing: it was all worked out by OPAck and logarithms. But where British officers would say: "Two degrees to the right. Fire. Jolly good, you're on target." The American officers would yell: "Say boy you're knocking shit out of 'em. Keep going. Keep going!" And Eddy would have no idea how many rounds to fire or at what.

They introduced the Yanks to sardines and oxtail soup – and they loved them. Most of the US troops went around with a large bag of cigarettes trying to swap them for liberated German Luger pistols. But Eddy and the other gunners got them to swap their fags for sardines and oxtail soup.

Yank discipline was terrible. They lost more men than they needed just through being stupid. They had big old Brownings. Every night the Germans – not so many that half as many British soldiers couldn't have cleared them, and the Yanks were supposed to be waiting for reinforcements – rattled a few stones in a tin. It was the oldest gag going. And the Yanks fell for it every time. Every night one of them opened up – the low steady beat of the Browning. Eddy's crew dug their slit trench deeper. Because every night, a half hour after the Yanks had opened fire, the Germans, having now got a fix on their position, mortared them.

The next morning the American Colonel came down, called them all "cocksucking lowdown bastards ..." Eddy and the others couldn't believe their ears. But it didn't cure them.

The Colonel said to Eddy: "We won't have enough men to advance at all if this goes on." The Colonel came from Illinois. "What happens in your mob when you're like this?"

"It's different altogether, Sir."

"No need to call me Sir. I'm only a colonel."

"Your blokes call you Sir."

"But they don't mean it."

The Yanks did have discipline, could be given up to twenty years in military prison for almost anything. But you could see, with a bit of sense, where The Bullshit came in. With all of them allowed to voice an opinion, they ended up doing nothing and catching a packet from the Germans. Whereas, in the British Army, you did as you were told; unless you had a bad officer, then you said 'yes' and used your loaf. The Yanks, though, didn't have that sort of discipline; and their officers appeared to hold life cheap – there were so many of them. American officers seemed to have the same attitude towards their troops that the British Generals had possessed in the Great War. Patten was the worst. The Yanks all hated him.

One day the whole American front opened up. Assuming that the Germans had started a counter-attack, Eddy yelled: "Take post!"

They got up to the gun only to find that the Yanks were all firing at a hare going across the field in front. Brownings, rifles, the lot. And they never hit it.

When Eddy left them, the 11th Armoured had still been trying to push through Holland. The Germans, as they retreated, had left behind several self-propelled guns and tanks with enough ammunition and provisions to be able to operate on their own. These isolated units were allowing the combat troops to pass and then shooting up the soft vehicles – supply wagons and petrol tankers. They were making a mess of Allied planning.

C troop was sent back to search out those guns. They got a few of them, but it was a difficult task. The Germans knocked out two of the London Yeomanry and one of C troop's guns. Luckily the men weren't hurt.

Eddy rejoined the advancing Guards Armoured division. But German forces counter-attacked and managed to cut the road. Eddy's company was in the middle of the cut. He could see his infantry down the road, and they could see him, but he didn't dare move, and so kept his gun hidden by a church tower. Had he moved, the Germans would have knocked him out. When the Germans tried to use the road he knocked them out instead.

Both sides stayed hidden and used indirect fire. The Germans had the advantage – they had an observer in the church tower, and Eddy's lot couldn't get at him. Because of him, on the next gun to Eddy, Bombardier MacGilligan and Sergeant Eyelett copped it. They had got out of their gun and a shell exploded beside them. MacGilligan had received a telegram the day before. His first baby had been born. MacGilligan was blown in half.

He had been a bit of a toff, had a brother well up in the Navy. A nice man, but proper Army – never went out with other women, never drank. His sole priority had been the child that was to be born.

Shells were pitching alongside Eddy's gun too, but his crew stayed in the gun and kept firing, and were lucky. Except for Lazenby, who did jump out of the gun. He received twenty-three pieces of shrapnel in him; and Carrington got a little bit in his finger. Luckily none of the twenty-three pieces in Lazenby was serious.

Their position was hopeless but, before they retreated, Eddy and Sergeant Merrith buried MacGilligan and Eyelett.

They got out of there with the help of a Dutch farmer. It was deadly when night came. They could hear the shrapnel zinging along the side of the gun. And to start the gun's engine once it had been stopped a couple of days they had to get out and crank it manually with a big handle.

The Dutch farmer had told the officers that if they could get the guns going he would lead them out towards friendly lines. He went first in a Bren carrier. By the time they moved around behind the German guns it was dawn.

As they headed for the allied line, they spotted an American anti-tank gun on a bridge. Eddy and the rest doubted that the Yanks had seen a British self-propelled gun before, so they came down that road letting off yellow flares and shouting for all they were worth. When they reached the bridge the Yanks said: "By gawd we almost let you have it there."

To reach his cut-off infantry Eddy's troop still had to go back through German lines. The next town was half held by Yanks and half by Germans, with – in the middle – a narrow bridge over the river. The self-propelled guns had to run the gauntlet through that town. Once they were on the other side of the town, they weren't far from the German tanks and guns that had cut the road.

Major Hart had taken bearings on the German positions before they left the church tower. So they now lined up the eight self-propelled guns, and shelled the German tanks and guns until the road was opened up again. Unfortunately, apart from some armour piercing rounds, they were out of ammunition.

They sat nervously by some woods on the other side of that town waiting for the ammo to come up, hoping that the Germans didn't counter-attack.

During the day, the guns well hidden, they patrolled on foot with rifles and Stens. They were walking through the woods on one such patrol when they heard noises. Three of them crept along, and down in a dell saw a few German soldiers eating tins of pork and peas. Eddy and the others had a good look at them, then quietly crept off again. They didn't know how many more Germans might have been concealed in that area, while they had eight mobile guns with not one round of ammunition between them that would have been of any use against infantry. They told the officer, called Gay, what they had seen. He was nervous: they could do nothing.

Dutch people in a nearby farm gave them tea. They were short of food themselves; but they offered Dutch money for boots. The Canadians, when they advanced, dug up dead Germans for their boots. When Eddy's troop came across any Germans who had surrendered to the Canadians, the Germans would say: "*Alles kaput.* Canadians." Many were left with just a pair of pants.

The Canadians took everything they thought they could sell, and had learned there was a shortage of boots in Holland. The Canadians ahead of Eddy's crowd had cleared the roads with help from Typhoon fighter-bomber rocket fire.

The Germans had buried their dead in the road verges. And by the time Eddy came to use the road, all he could see along its verges were bare, blackened feet sticking out of the ground where the Canadians had taken the boots.

Eddy was again attached to the Guards Armoured to capture a big bridge between Hoos and Nijmegen. They took it intact. And while the paratroopers were fighting for their lives in Arnhem – against a crack SS Panzer Division, where they had been told to expect only a few low grade troops – Eddy spent days fighting in Nijmegen.

One battle was fought in a fur coat factory. Everybody, including the Germans, ended up fighting in fur coats. It was so cold.

Meanwhile, at Arnhem, some of the Dorsets were sent in to try to rescue the paratroopers. They had to cross the river in small boats. Only nine men came out of that alive. However, once

Nijmegen was captured, the Germans were soon pushed out of Arnhem. But it was too late for the British paratroopers, and the hoped-for break-through across the Rhine and into Germany from Arnhem never happened.

Nijmegen was in the hilly part of Holland. From above Nijmegen they could look down on Germany. It was like a little Haldon Moor up there; and they were given a small terraced house in Nijmegen, could go down from the moor for two or three days rest. The local brewery had a bar put up in the house for them.

In the centre of Nijmegen was a huge glass place; looked like it could have been a botanical garden once. Any soldier who went in there was given twenty cigarettes free and a cup of tea. They were served by girls whose heads had been shaved for collaborating. In the mornings the girls were brought from the jail all tied to a long rope. And after they had been all day serving they were tied to the rope again and taken back to the jail. The soldiers didn't like it, felt embarrassed being served by the poor little maids with their shaven heads.

In Nijmegen Eddy found himself with his whole regiment for the first time since D-Day. He met Colonel Fenshaw for the first time since the New Forest. He had been promoted to Brigadier.

"I'm n-n-not enamoured with NCOs," Brigadier Fenshaw said, "who put people on charges. But you B-B-Bombadier; I don't know how you do it. You've never had a man on a charge. Must be a record for the British Army. That Scotchman we had from Dundee – he went from every gun in the regiment until he ended up with you. Then he got himself posted. Bit of a do over that, was there?"

"We had a few words, Sir, one afternoon," Eddy said. "And I had no uniform on." Brigadier Fenshaw laughed in response.

Eddy liked Fenshaw. As far as Eddy was concerned he was the man responsible for them suffering only a quarter of the casualties they would have had under anyone else. He hadn't asked the men to go anywhere that he hadn't been. But his jeep driver had gone bald very quickly.

From Nijmegen, they could see the big German guns firing from the Siegfried line and two Big Berthas. Eddy's lot called those the Nijmegen Express – 500mm. They could hear the shells going over above them, see them burst behind them in Nijmegen. And from the moors, they saw aerial dogfights.

The Germans had jets. The Allies did not. The gunners would see the vapour trails miles up, and then a little white spot as the parachute came down. Nothing they could do on the ground: the Bofors gun was useless against jets. So, the Allied fighter tactic was to air-patrol near the German bases and shoot down the jets as they slowed to land.

After Nijmegen, they were given a dangerous little job out towards Gillerhosen, which again was hilly for Holland. A bulldozer came up and dug them in – all twenty-four guns. They were there to knock out some German mortars. Whenever the mortars opened up so would all twenty-four guns, and knock hell out of them. One crowd, though, wouldn't budge. So Eddy's troop was ordered up. The Germans could not help but hear the four guns coming towards them. They had to be lying in wait for them. Luckily, C troop was ordered back before they reached the German positions.

In Northern Holland, there were a lot of infiltrators. In one place a monk in cowl and habit came up to their gun and asked for a shell casing as a souvenir. Mac didn't trust anybody. Two or three hours after the monk's visit, they were shelled. They moved from there. The monk came up to them again. Again they were shelled.

"I've tumbled that bastard," Mac said. "He's a bloody Jerry informer."

The next time the monk came up they grabbed hold of him behind the gun, whipped off his cowl and habit, and told him that if he didn't confess they would stick him on the ground and run the tracks over him. Carrington hopped into the gun and revved the engine, edged the gun backwards a little bit.

The monk confessed. He was of German descent, an informer, and was spotting for their artillery. Eddy handed him over to the Dutch resistance. The monk begged them not to – the resistance didn't keep prisoners. The resistance shot him.

Eddy could not sleep while anything was going on. If they were firing on a fixed target he would stay up nights on his own, fire the gun, let the others sleep. One night an officer asked him how long he had been doing night guards. Eddy told him that he had been doing it every night for two weeks. The officer ordered him to go to sleep. Eddy leant against a brick wall and slept.

On the German border, they came up against Germany's Home Guard – old men and boys. They were holding a strong defensive position, but the Allies just blitzed it and walked through. Eddy recalled when he had been in the Home Guard and was called out to repel the invasion, Vera sending him off with a bag of sandwiches. He realised now that had it been a real invasion he would have stood about as much chance as the German Home Guard – nil.

The Germans held out in Hertogenbosch for quite a while. The Allies had by-passed it on the way to Nijmegen. Eddy was sent back to give artillery support, was firing from about four miles. The infantry and tanks found an old disused railway track and went along it into what, in Britain, would have been a low-cost council housing estate. And in that council estate, the battle for Hertogenbosch was fought.

They went back to Hoos, which was a town about the size of Ashburton in England, and parked the gun in a brickyard. The countryside was flat. Eddy decided to go for a walk. As usual, he took his Sten with him. He preferred a Sten to a rifle.

He walked. It was twilight. A man came along.

"How do you do?" he said.

"How do you do?" Eddy said.

"Where are you going?" the man asked.

"Back to Hoos. Been for a walk."

"You're behind German lines here," the man said. He was a Dutch farmer's son, wanted Eddy to go back to the farm for a drink. Eddy was suspicious, said thank you but he would carry on.

"When you get two miles up the road be careful," the man said. "The Dutch resistance have a post there."

That put the wind up Eddy more than knowing he was behind German lines. The resistance did not take prisoners. However, when he did reach the post, they took him in, questioned him and sent him on to their headquarters, where they questioned him some more. Eddy told them that he had helped the French resistance. The Dutch gave him a good booze-up.

Sixteen

October 28th 1944 – May 8th 1945

November 10th-11th 1944: Kweilin and Liuchnow taken by Japanese. British troops launch campaign against Greek communists.

November 24th 1944: First USAAF raid on Tokyo.

December 2nd 1944: Home Guard stood down.

December 16th 1944: (until January 16th 1945) Battle of the Bulge.

December 18th 1944: Japanese in Hangkow bombed by USAAF. Germans reach Stavelot.

December 25th 1944: Churchill and Eden impose provisional government on Greece. Allies take Pelelin. Allies take Leyte.

January 12th 1945: Cuzon taken by Allies.

January 15th 1945: Russians take Kieke.

January 16th 1945: Russians take Radom.

January 17th 1945: Russians take Warsaw.

January 19th 1945: Russians take Cracow.

January 20th 1945: Russians reach German soil.

January 21st 1945: Russians take Insterburg.

January 23rd 1945: Russians take Bromberg and Kalisz.

January 31st 1945: Russians take Landsberg.

February 1945: Russians forty miles from Berlin.

February 11th 1945: Yalta Conference.

February 13th 1945: Russians take Somerfeld and Budapest.

February 14th 1945: Dresden bombed.

February 16th-17th 1945: Tokyo bombed.

February 23rd 1945: Poznam taken by Russians.

March 3rd 1945: US wins Battle of Manila.

March 9th-10th 1945: Mass Allied raids on Tokyo (84,000 killed). US troops cross Rhine. Laskio, Mandalay and Meiktilia back in British hands. Iwo Jima taken by Allies.

March 21st 1945: Patten crosses Rhine at Oppenheim.

March 23rd 1945: 2nd Army crosses Rhine en route to Ruhr.

March 27th 1945: Last V2.

March 28th 1945: Montgomery twenty miles over Rhine.

March 29th 1945: Last V1.

April 1945: Belsen and Buchenwald discovered.

April 9th 1945: Allied Italian offensive begins.

April 11th 1945: Allied armies reach Elbe.

April 12th 1945: Roosevelt dies.

April 19th 1945: British take Kyaupedaung.

April 14th 1945: Allies take Bastia Bridge.

April 16th 1945: Indian Corps take Taungup.

April 19th 1945: Allies take Chauk.

April 20th 1945: Allies take Magwe.

April 21st 1945: Allies take Yenangyaung.

April 26th 1945: British take Toungoo.

April 27th 1945: US and USSR armies meet at Elbe. British cross the Padige.

April 28th 1945: Mussolini and his mistress are hung from meathooks in Milan.

April 29th 1945: German Armies in Italy surrender.

April 30th 1945: Adolf Hitler and Eva Braun commit suicide.

May 3rd 1945: British troops enter Rangoon.

May 4th 1945: Germans in NW Europe surrender.

May 7th 1945: German Supreme Command surrenders at Rheims.
May 8th 1945: VE day.

Vera began her labour pains at eleven o'clock in the morning on 28th October 1944. Doll took her to the hospital in a taxi.

Vera hadn't received a letter from Eddy for two months, although she assumed he was alive because she was still getting his Army pay. After the first month of no letters she had contacted the Families Association and they had tried to discover his whereabouts. But all they could tell her was that Eddy's regiment had been advancing. They didn't know where.

Because her husband was away, Vera had had to go to the ante-natal clinic for unmarried mothers. She had kept on working at Maison Vee's until too big to work any longer. Rene was now in charge.

The confinement was difficult. Two Sisters ministered to Vera. Four times they tried to deliver the baby with forceps.

One of the Sisters said to the Matron: "We really should call the doctor."

"I have delivered thousands of babies," the Matron said. "I have a reputation. And I'm not going to have a doctor. I haven't had a doctor for any one of my confinements, and I have no intention of calling one now."

Vera pushed; and still the baby didn't come. Exhausted, she saw herself – as if she was looking down from the ceiling – lying on the bed, saw herself leaking wet with sweat, her hair sticking to her face, thought, *Don't I look awful.*

At ten o'clock in the morning, October 29th, the baby arrived at last.

"He's got a hare lip," the Matron announced.

"It's not a hare lip, Matron," the Sister argued. "It's just a cleft lip."

"More or less the same," the Matron snapped.

Vera was too numb; too glad it was over, too tired to care.

On October 29th, 1944, Eddy was still in the brickyard in Hoos. The snow was deep. It was ice cold. With the ground frozen, they had to feed Wilfred, their rabbit, on biscuits, square chipolatas from a tin, baked beans and boiled sweets.

Eddy had been drinking rum. He passed Dad Barlowe in a trench counting out French letters. He was a dirty old bugger, but kept quiet about it, just used to slip off. By rights, Dad Barlowe should have stayed in England: he was too old – forty now. But as Battery Sergeant Major, he had been too valuable to leave behind.

During the hectic action of the past few months, Eddy had been able to ignore his backache from the shell blast in Normandy. But now, even with a bellyful of rum, the pain was excruciating as he walked. He collapsed, unconscious.

When he woke up in the snow he spat out a lump of blood that looked like a piece of liver. He called out and the others found him. Mac gave him a cup of tea and fetched Dad Barlowe. They stuck him up on a half-track and took him down to an old farmhouse that was being used as a field station.

There they tied a yellow tag to him and sent him to the other side of Hertogenbosch. His back was as stiff as a plank, his left leg numb and cold. One lung wasn't working. The medics, thinking he had pneumonia, gave him a shot of penicillin. He was then loaded onto a plane and flown to Eindhoven.

Mac and Dad had put his rings in his bag and sent it with him from Hoos. But by the time he got to Eindhoven all he had left was a razor and a pair of civilian shoes. The Medical Corps couldn't get any first-hand loot so they looted the wounded.

Everybody had a racket.

Vera was put in a ward with eighteen other new mothers. Every woman there, except Vera, had her husband with her. Other soldiers had been given compassionate leave. Vera still had no real idea whether Eddy was alive or dead.

When the husbands came at visiting time the nurses drew the curtains around Vera's bed. Her bed was between two others. The curtains went right up to the ceiling and cut out the light. So, at visiting times, Vera lay there alone, unable to read, listening to all the kissing and chatter on either side of her.

Doll asked if she could visit Vera. But the hospital had a rule – only husbands allowed. Vera was left on her own; and the baby was fading away before her eyes. As soon as she put him to her breast, he pulled air in through the slit in his top lip.

All the women in her ward seemed to have had difficult births. The girl who lived opposite her in Congella – her baby had died inside her, had come out in bits and pieces. Another baby had a crooked spine – that one lived. Another baby's stomach wasn't connected to its throat, had to be operated on immediately. Another girl's baby died as it was being born. And, as if to make matters worse, nothing was wrong with any of the unmarried mothers' unwanted babies upstairs.

For three days Vera lay on her back while the other new mothers were up and about. Except for feeding time, the baby was taken from her and kept in the nursery with the other babies. A ward sister, a calm woman although a spinster, was kind and sympathetic to Vera. The Matron came along.

"You can go up and have a bath now," she told Vera.

"She's not fit," the sister objected. "She hasn't been out of bed yet."

"Of course she's fit," the Matron snapped.

Two of the sisters helped Vera up to the bath. Her anxiety over the baby, over Eddy, over being the only woman there who didn't get visitors, was making her shake all over. But she lowered herself into the bath. She felt herself fainting off, felt the water sliding up over her face; and she thought – *it doesn't matter.* And immediately another thought – *what's going to happen to the baby?* She reached for the bell above the bath. The next thing she knew, Doll was by her bedside.

After Vera had been in hospital a week, Doll asked if she could take her home. When Ned and her mother saw Vera and the baby, they both broke down in tears.

In Eindhoven a doctor examined Eddy and another man with a hole in his guts and said they were too ill to travel to England. All the other sick and injured who had arrived in Eindhoven with Eddy were sent back to England. But Eddy was held overnight and was then put on a Dakota and flown to Brussels.

The army's forward hospital in Brussels had marble staircases and floors. Patients were only allowed to stay there a month. They had Belgian nurses and English sisters.

Eddy was so used to the roar of the gun and the crack of its firing, along with the constant tension of the front line, that the peace and quiet of the hospital unnerved him. After only a week – time to recall all his narrow escapes, time to think what could have happened – he was suffering from combat exhaustion. It was very common. The combat exhaustion was worse than his back.

He was so weak now that he couldn't lift his arm. The doctors told him that the muscles in his back had all gone out of shape. Eddy had thought that his backache had been lumbago. And everyone had naturally been very jumpy so he hadn't paid any attention to his nerves. The wards were so very quiet, though, that they made the noise of the V1s going overhead even more terrifying.

Eddy was graded down with chronic battle fatigue. He was more annoyed about it than anything. Having made it this far, he had wanted to see it through to the end. The regiment had been bound for Bremen when he collapsed. The doctors, though, couldn't understand how he had managed to keep on fighting for as long as he had. His regiment had originally been trained to go for three months: they had been fighting flat out for six.

There were stacks more men flap-happy in the hospital. Most of them were taken to the loony bin in Brussels. The sweats were the worst – dehydrated them.

When the baby was fed he sucked in air through the slit in his lip, got terrible colic. Vera went to see her cousins, who had some money. They knew doctors. She took the baby to her own family doctors, Jacobs and Lee. Jacobs tried everywhere. But most of the plastic surgeons were away working on men wounded in the war. No-one had time for one small baby with a split lip.

Vera still had no idea whether Eddy was alive or dead. Jacobs asked her if she would have the operation done privately.

" 'Course I will," Vera said.

It would cost over one hundred pounds. Their house had cost them seven hundred. She would have to go into hospital with the baby, and so she would have to pay for herself too. The operation alone would cost a hundred pounds, without the charge for the use of the operating theatre, the private room, the anaesthetic and her meals.

The baby was operated on. All that Vera had to do all day long was to pump out her milk. But the pumps that the hospital had were so old that they didn't work properly. The rubber had perished; and, because of the war, could not be replaced. After surgery, the baby wasn't allowed to suck. Vera had to spoonfeed him. He went blue with wind. But on no account was he to cry in case he broke his stitches. They gave him drugs to keep him quiet.

After a month in Brussels, Eddy was carried onto a train and taken to the base hospital in Amiens. When he arrived, the boys in his ward told him that he had to go up and see the Glamour Girl.

She was a Major, about thirty-two, a peach. Two male nurses had taken Eddy up on a stretcher. She carried on writing, said: "Be with you in a minute, Bombardier. Don't suppose you've got the strength to take off your pyjamas."

"No," Eddy said.

She undid his pyjama bottoms, pulled his pants down, and started rubbing her hand all around his genitals. There wasn't life enough in Eddy to get a stand.

"This the leg that goes cold?" she asked him.

"Yes," Eddy said.

She had a small pair of scissors in her hand. She stuck the point in his leg. Eddy felt nothing. She prodded away at his leg, asking him questions, then suddenly she jabbed the scissors right in his leg, drawing blood. Eddy still felt nothing. He heard afterwards that one blade of the scissors was sharp and the other blunt, and so they soon found out if anyone was malingering.

An old Scots Colonel from the last war was in charge of the hospital – a right bastard. He didn't believe in combat exhaustion, thought they were all swinging the lead. The Matron was a last war woman too. She had an Eton crop, always had a ciggy hanging from her lip. Of Eddy's ward she said: "Can't do anything with these dead-end kids."

Each patient was given a white shirt, blue waistcoat, a white pair of pants, blue trousers, white vest and blue coat. That all had to be packed in the bedside locker with a red tie coming down the exact centre of the pile. And in all the other wards when the Matron came around the men had to lie at attention. The men in Eddy's ward, though, couldn't do that, couldn't be upset. They habitually insulted the Matron.

One of the men in Eddy's ward looked as fit as a fiddle. He had nine children. The Ward sister was a sod too – everything had to be clean and tidy. One day he said to the sister: "Ward Sister."

"Yes, Johnston?"

"Have you seen my wife and family?" He had their photographs on his locker.

"I'm not blind Johnston. 'Course I can see your wife and family."

"Well if they were here, heard you speak to me the way you do, all the lot of 'em would kick your fuckin' teeth in."

There was nothing she could do about it – the man was sick.

They had one doctor in Amiens who was on their side: he had been a prisoner of war. He wrote reams about each patient every morning. Eddy kept bringing his food up as soon as he ate it. The ward sister didn't believe him. The doctor ordered her to give Eddy a bowl to be sick into. She didn't. So Eddy kept his porridge bowl back and was sick into that. When the doctor came round he asked Eddy if he'd been sick and if he'd kept it, Eddy told him that he had. The ward sister said that he couldn't have been sick, as he didn't have a bowl.

"He should have," the doctor said. "My instructions to you, Sister, were to leave him a bowl."

"I did it in my porridge bowl, Sir," Eddy said.

The doctor gave her hell. The patients were not to be upset. The slightest worry could bring them out in a sweat, and that might kill them. In other wards no-one was allowed to sleep when the doctor came on his rounds. In the dead-end kids' ward they slept on regardless.

One of the men in Eddy's ward had almost become a doctor. He was a university type, tall and gangly. The other men would ask him about their complaints and he'd look it up for them. His was nerves. Another man in there had two lots of teeth, should never have been allowed in the Army at all, and was as nutty as they came. He'd been brought in off a convoy as it passed through Amiens and hadn't been in the Army long.

In the bed next to Eddy was a Canadian. He got double-O rations – twice as much as Eddy got. He was a fine boy. In the bed the other side was a Scottish boy; and then there was Old Bradford.

Most of the infantry in there had big wounds down their backs from mortar shells. The Scottish boy's nerves were bad. He was a Spanish-Glaswegian – his mother and father had a fish and chip shop in Glasgow. He could speak fluent Spanish, and English in broad Glaswegian. He used to sing. The terrible sweats from battle exhaustion affected the heart. The Spanish-Glaswegian died.

Old Bradford was about thirty-eight – he just looked older. He'd been left out alone in Tillberg in Holland in a trench and they hadn't been able to get a counter-attack going to get him back. For three days and three nights he'd stayed out there, had developed double pneumonia. He held the record for the most penicillin anyone had ever had. He got out of bed and went to the lavatory when he shouldn't have. It killed him. That small exertion had been too much for his heart.

Doll came to the hospital to see Vera one night. She sat with her, said hardly a word. Vera wondered what the matter could be.

Before Doll had come in to see Vera and the baby she had to wait in the nurses' room. The baby's file had happened to be open on top of the desk. On it had been written that the bottom stitch had gone septic and would have to be removed. It was the most important stitch. The doctor who had done the operation had been seventy years old.

When Eddy began to get better, could get up and about, the Scots Colonel told him: "I think you're fit enough to go back up the front."

"Do you know anything about the front?" Eddy asked him.

"What do you mean?"

"I'd rather go back to my regiment than be down here with you lot any day," Eddy said. "But I'm not fit to take responsibility. And when you've got five men on a gun you're responsible for their lives."

The Scots Colonel sent Eddy instead to a convalescent depot in St Pol. St Pol was an important railway centre something like Swindon back home. Eddy and two other patients walked into Major Woodward's office. He looked them over. "My Christ, where've you come from?"

"The 88th," Eddy said.

"Amiens, I suppose?"

"Yes Sir."

The Major looked up to his sergeant. "They'll be coming down here in wooden waistcoats in a minute. All we'll have to do is screw 'em down."

He put the three of them into a little ward on their own, told them to stay in there, that someone would bring them grub, and that they could go out, or not, as they pleased. And every day Major Woodward came to see them. Three times he judged Eddy not fit enough to be in the convalescent home and sent him back to Amiens. And each time that Eddy went back he fell out with the Scots Colonel.

They had a night nurse in Amiens, a girl from Cumberland. She was having an affair with the Canadian boy. Night times, Eddy heard them behind the curtains puffing and blowing.

One morning Eddy woke up with a sore arm, wondered what he'd been up to in the night. Quite often, when he was delirious in the night, the medical staff injected him with drugs to knock him out. This particular morning the Cumberland nurse came along, "You enjoy yourself last night then, Bombardier?"

"Don't know. Why?" Eddy asked her.

"I had a lovely time," she said. "Down at the Globe Hotel with Frank Andrews and you."

"Globe Hotel?"

"In Newton Abbot. We had a lovely time. In the band, all the girls you knew, the men you introduced me to ..."

"What the hell are you talking about?"

"We only just caught you. You were down the drive in your pyjamas, snow everywhere. I don't know how you got out of the hospital, past all the orderlies ..."

Eddy had no memory of any of this. But, apparently, he often did things like that; and it worried him, not knowing why he did it, and why he couldn't remember it.

Major Woodward of St Pol sent Eddy to Lille to see a Canadian specialist. Three of them went in an ambulance. On their way there, the Battle of the Bulge began. Lille was directly in the German path. Every convalescent capable of carrying a gun was given one. The ambulance had to pull in under some trees as German planes strafed the road.

Canadians were stationed in Lille. Canadians were very smart – uniforms always pressed, pleats everywhere – more bull than in the British Army. The Canadian specialist couldn't see the three of them until after lunch. He told his aide to kit them out and give them a good feed. They were given overcoats, double kit of everything else, and didn't have to sign for any of it. Boots as well – a full kit bag. And if they didn't use it they could sell it. By the time they had eaten, it was half past two.

The specialist did the usual – first he examined Eddy's fingernails, turned the hands over, and then looked into the corner of his eyes. Then Eddy was laid down on the bed and stripped, and the specialist tested all his reflexes.

"Right Bombardier," the specialist said. "Give me your paybook." Eddy handed it over.

"Right, C1. That's it. Nobody can grade you up unless they're the same rank as me. And there isn't a lot of us. Now you can go back. You'll have to see that old bastard Scots Colonel, and go in front of a board, but there's nothing they can do about it. All they can do is sign this paybook."

Eddy told him there had been several rows between him and the Colonel.

"Well you'll just be able to sit there and smirk now, boy. Won't ya?"

The specialist asked Eddy what he did in civilian life. Eddy told him that he was a bricklayer.

"I dunno. You might be able to do bricklaying again. But it'll serve you hard to start with. What do you do for a hobby?"

"I play in a band. Semi-pro. It's a sort of paying hobby. And I like to do bit of fishing."

"Ah," the specialist said. "When you go home, boy, and you get this acute melancholia come over you, you take that trowel and throw it one way, and you take that hammer and throw it the other way, and you take your fishing rod and you go and sit on that rock. And if you can beat it that way, don't go on the drugs. Because you'll never beat it that way."

Eddy went back to Amiens.

Vera didn't sleep much in hospital. The Matron told her to go out for a walk. Vera wandered up towards Hele village. She still didn't know if Eddy was alive or dead. She fainted outside a chemist's shop. Next thing she knew she was back in hospital; and they laughed at her because she couldn't have chosen a better place to pass out.

On Christmas day, they said that the baby could go home. The hospital took him off the drug keeping him quiet. But at home, the baby wouldn't take anything. At five o'clock, they still hadn't had their Christmas dinner. And the baby was turning grey. Vera tried spoonfeeding him, but it just dribbled out the side of his mouth. He was like a little old man.

"That dear little bugger's dying," Ned said. "Feed him! Feed him yourself."

"Dad I can't," Vera said. "His stitches'll rip. They told me when I came out that on no account must he be breastfed."

"Don't matter if he breaks the bloody stitches," Ned said. "He's going to die else."

Vera fed him. Expecting the blood to come spurting out at any moment she watched the stitches. But the babe sucked and sucked, and as he sucked, the colour came back to him. And that night, for the first time in his life, he slept a whole night without whimpering.

Meanwhile Doll had been phoning the hospital, telling them that the baby was going a funny colour, could he be breastfed? On no account, the hospital told her. Doll told them that she didn't think the baby would last the night. Nonsense, they told her.

The next day Vera and Doll took the baby out to the hospital. The Matron looked into the pram.

"And is this the little boy who's supposed to be dying?"

"He's better now," Vera said.

"You haven't fed him, have you?"

"Oh no," Vera said. And she continued to breastfeed him, even though the stitches in his lips tore at her breasts.

Eddy spent Christmas in St Pol.

Back again in Amiens the Colonel actually accused Eddy of swinging the lead.

"No fucker's ever said that to me," Eddy said.

"What did you call me?"

"I said no fucker's ever said that to me. I've never been called a bloody coward in my life. After what I been through, who the bloody hell are you to call me a coward? Sat back here, a bloody Colonel from the last war, a medical bloke. You're out of date, you. Even the major where I've come from says you're no bloody good."

"I'll have you fall in!" he shouted.

"You can't do nothing," Eddy said. And the colonel couldn't do anything, not with Eddy's combat fatigue.

Vera took the baby to hospital to have his stitches removed.

"Quick, catch hold of him," the nurse said, "while I take out this stitch." Vera fainted again. When she got the baby home, and now that she could see the result of the operation, she wasn't too pleased. The baby's nose was crooked and his top lip was out of shape. She took the baby to Dr Jacobs.

"Can't I have something done? I'm sure this isn't right."

"When he's fourteen you won't notice it, Mrs Dart."

"Isn't there anyone else I can go to? Anything?"

"There's no need to worry, my dear."

In Amiens, clergymen of all cloths had visited Eddy. He had told an old Welsh Baptist minister that he hadn't heard from Vera. The Baptist minister had written to the Reverend Robinson in Ellacombe. The Reverend Robinson visited Vera. He told her that Eddy was safe, although he was in hospital.

Vera wept with relief.

Back in Amiens, Eddy received his first letters from Vera in four months. The ones she had written earlier about the birth were missing. He couldn't make out what was wrong with the baby, why the baby should be in hospital. He wrote to ask her; but, before he got a reply, he was again sent to St Pol.

Vera received a pile of Eddy's letters – scraps of paper barely legible, written in a hurry when he'd been advancing, saying that he was alright, hoped that she was alright. All of them were months old, except for the last one, which said that he was glad she was safe but what did she mean about the little boy going into hospital? What was wrong with him?

So she had to write telling him all over again what had happened. Doll wrote the letter for her. She enclosed a photo. Eddy could just make out a mark on the baby's upper lip.

From St Pol, Eddy was sent to Hasselt. In Hasselt he was put in charge of a dining room next to a big prison where anybody – Yanks, Canadians – could come for a meal.

In Hasselt, they had a diphtheria epidemic. The diphtheria itself didn't actually kill the men; it was the state of feebleness it left them in. If they did not stay on their backs for weeks afterwards, then, like Old Bradford, the exertion killed them.

Eddy was in Hasselt on VE day.

Seventeen

May 1945 – 1946

May 23rd 1945: Churchill resigns. Most of New Guinea under Allied control.

June 2nd 1945: Allies take Okinawa.

July 5th 1945: Attlee wins General Election.

July 20th 1945: British slaughter Japanese at Siltang River.

July 26th 1945: Potsdam Conference: Stalin, Attlee, Bevin, Truman and Chiang Kai'chek present.

August 6th 1945: Atom bomb dropped on Hiroshima (70,000 killed).

August 9th 1945: Atom bomb dropped on Nagasaki (200,000 killed). Russia invades Manchuria.

August 14th 1945: Japan surrenders.

September 2nd 1945: Emperor Hirohito formally surrenders.

September 9th 1945: Okamura surrenders China to Ho Ying-Chin.

September 10th 1945: Rear Admiral Sato surrenders.

September 12th 1945: Japan surrenders to Mountbatten at Singapore. VJ Day.

September 13th 1945: General Adachi surrenders at Wom.

Eddy was sent to a rehabilitation unit in Bruges, a Medieval Belgian town. He had to stay there until he was given a posting. The unit was run by Pioneers.

There were scores of convalescent men in Bruges. Most of them were put on courses to become clerks. The Army needed clerks in Japan. Eddy didn't want to go to Japan – the war was still going on there. So he got himself sent from Bruges to Ghent.

Ghent was another Medieval town. It had a racecourse and a huge mill. The only other mill Eddy had seen its size had been in Dumfries. All the troops stayed in the mill.

The Army had sent instructors out from England to give them machine gun drill, keep them occupied. All the men would troop up after the instructor, the instructor would start, and all the men would just walk away and go down the town. The soldiers knew back to front what the instructors were telling them – they had been using the bloody things for real.

In the town, if they didn't have a red lanyard – signifying they were staff – the townspeople automatically assumed that they were a little mad. The soldiers played up to this assumption. Eddy and six others would go into a café, order a drink, and play cards – without money, without cards. Four Scotsmen were always leading an invisible horse through the town. The local police would take pity on them.

"*Sal de guerre. Sal de guerre.*"

And the traffic would be held up until the non-existent horse had passed.

One day they were sent to a mill, about two miles away on the other side of town. The regimental sergeant major over there was a graded down Guards sergeant. He came to take them over. He was a big man with a ginger moustache, carried a pace stick. He lined them all up exactly, issued them with full pack and rifle, and drilled them. He made them stand to attention, at ease, attention, at ease.

"Sod this," Eddy said to the bloke next to him. "I'm going to drop my rifle next time." Dropping a rifle on parade was a cardinal offence. They came to attention, sloped arms, and just as the officer who was to take them over arrived – clatter, bang, wallop – Eddy dropped his rifle.

The Sergeant arrived in front of him, began to bawl him out. The officer shook his head. The Sergeant stamped away. The officer came over to Eddy.

"Why did you drop your rifle?"

"I can't hold it up, Sir. Not after an hour. What with a big pack and that. I've had shell blast. It's all in my medical report. And I'm C1. What with that and my nerves ..."

"C1? You're not supposed to have a rifle are you?"

"No Sir. Not really."

"Put your rifle and pack up on the three-tonner and ride over on that."

Eddy was sent next to Overijse, about ten miles outside Brussels. It was a vast prisoner of war camp. The Major in charge of the camp – Major Bowie – had only one eye. He had lost the other in Burma.

He told the new arrivals: "We've got you boys here because you've all been in action. And been graded down. Up until now this camp has been staffed by men straight out from England. And the Germans were running the camp. So we've got you boys here to take over the compounds and put a stop to it."

Eddy was given Number Two Compound. Number Two Compound was about a mile long. There were five thousand prisoners with two thousand of them going out to work every day. Eddy, Lionel and Old George were in charge of them all. Eddy, Lionel and Old George had a revolver and two rifles between them, plus a leather thong that Eddy carried attached to his wrist.

The German in charge of the Germans was called a *lagerfuhrer*. He was handsome man, a Nazi straight off German propaganda posters. *Well you bastard*, Eddy thought when he first saw him, *I'll soon tame you.*

The ordinary German servicemen were afraid to complain to the British soldiers because the Nazis would knock hell out of them. But Eddy got tipped off to investigate an area of the compound near the KZ tent – a small marquee holding German guards from the prisoner of war and concentration camps. Every so often Intelligence came and took a few away. Eddy would have preferred to shoot some of the bastards there and then.

Eddy reached the KZ marquee. Deep pits had been dug behind the marquee. Each pit was about twelve feet deep and six feet square. Inside each pit was a man.

This was the *lagerfuhrer's* punishment to his own men. The Germans were cruel to each other.

The men had been thrown a piece of bread and some water, had defecated in the pit, and had been in there about a week each. Their punishment was to last a fortnight. No-one else in the compound, even the colonel in charge, had known that it was happening.

Eddy was furious. He found the *lagerfuhrer*.

"Come with me."

"What's the matter?"

"You," Eddy said. "You're no longer SS. That's finished."

"You haven't got the authority." The *lagerfuhrer* knew his rights.

"Don't matter whether I got the authority or no. *Inleggen! Uffstand!* Lie down! Stand up!" The prisoners all around were watching. "Stand up! Lie down!" Eddy made him stand up, lie down on the path.

"I'll shoot the bastard," Old George said.

Old George came from Wiltshire. He'd been in Burma, was bomb-happy too.

"No. I'll take him down to the *straaflagar*." The British soldiers hated the British sergeant major in charge of their own detention centre – he was as bad as the Germans, as cruel as them. He'd come from an English glasshouse.

Eddy marched the *lagerfuhrer* down to the detention compound.

The *lagerfuhrer* could see that Eddy meant it, so went: "*Serek! Serek! Inleggen! Uffstand! Serek! Serek!*" all the way through three compounds to the detention centre.

Eddy told Sergeant Major Stone what he had found.

"Right!" Sergeant Major Stone yelled. Two Cockney soldiers were Sergeant Major Stone's assistants. First they sat the *lagerfuhrer* down and clipped off his hair. Then they strapped two boards to him, front and behind. Sergeant Major Stone did that to all his prisoners; then he made them nibble the grass on the little lawn that he had in front of his tent. Other times he lined his prisoners up in their boards, took up his squeezebox accordion and played the Blue Danube. Laa-la-la-la-la – bang bang, bang bang, he'd wallop the boards – Laa-la-la-la-la – bang bang, bang bang ...

Eddy showed the adjutant-colonel the pits. All the Nazis in the compound had decided to play up at the *lagerfuhrer* detention.

"What the hell shall we do, Bombardier?" the colonel asked Eddy.

"It's the sergeant really who should decide," Eddy said. But Sergeant Black never came up to the compound, was always in the mess.

"No good sending Sergeant Black up," the colonel said. "He doesn't know anything about it."

"Leave it to me then, Sir. Best thing to do, if they're going to behave like this, is stop their rations."

"We'll mount machine guns in the towers," the colonel said.

"No I don't want any of that." Eddy knew that the Belgian sentries would shoot the Germans at night just for going for a pee. "Unless they stop it, we'll just cut out their food."

The Germans only got enough food to keep them alive, and cooked it themselves in their own cookhouses. Their rations were stopped for four days; and each day Eddy paraded the prisoners in blocks of a hundred. Eddy, Lionel and Old George went around counting them. Difka, a German prisoner, also helped with the count. Many of the prisoners collapsed during these parades. Eddy got them picked up, only for them to collapse again. Four days was enough. The pits were filled in and the *lagerfuhrer* was transferred elsewhere.

Not long after this, Eddy was called down to the Regimental Office.

"I see you've got new war status, Bombardier."

"Yes Sir."

"Well you're due for leave. Two leaves in fact."

"Yes Sir. I've been trying to get it."

"Right then. I'll put you down for leave this weekend."

Eddy didn't have a chance to tell Vera he was coming home. He caught the train to Calais, and then the ferry to Folkestone. At Folkestone the returning soldiers didn't have to go through customs. Men were pushing pearl-grey prams piled high with loot along the breakwater. Eddy had not been out of hospital long enough to collect any.

He caught the overnight train from Folkestone, arrived in Torquay in the morning. In Congella Road, Vera opened the door to a complete stranger. She screamed.

Eddy immediately went upstairs to see his baby son. The boy was asleep. He had white blonde curly hair. In that darkened room Eddy stood looking down on him, and wept. Vera looked up at him from the bottom of the stairs, and wept, too. And the baby cried as well – awoken by this towering stranger weeping over him.

Vera studied Eddy. This wasn't the same man who had left her less than a year before. Then it had been a job to stop him talking. Now she couldn't get a word out of him.

In the days that followed, Vera looked at him and wondered who she had married. This wasn't Eddy. It was some stranger. He was quiet. They used to call him happy-go-lucky, irresponsible. One night in bed a Hurricane went over. He jumped out and dived under the bed, trembling all over. Other nights, out of his dreams, he shouted and screamed. Vera was frightened to wake him, frightened to tell her mother or Ned.

"Bastards!" Eddy would shout. "They've blown me up! My legs!" Or, "Who's that?" in the middle of the night. "That's poor old Harry gone."

"Get up for Chrissake!" He grabbed hold of Vera and pushed her down the bed.

They went for a walk with the baby, met Maud. Her husband hadn't gone. Good luck to him, Eddy would've said a year before. Maud's husband was now on war damage, working down Egerton Road.

"Cor, Eddy," Maud said. "You don't look half the bloke you did before you went in the Army."

"If your fuckin' old man," Eddy cracked off, "had been where I been he wouldn't look so bloody fat and good as he does."

Rene came round the house.

"Eddy!" she said and leapt at him to hug him. Eddy flinched. The sweat began pumping out of him. Vera was embarrassed.

"Hello Rene," Eddy said; and no more.

They went to the pictures. Eddy wasn't in there five minutes before he had to leave. There were many men like Eddy.

In the Overijse camp there were 98,000 Germans. If any hanged themselves, Eddy was the one who had to go and cut them down. The prisoners were naturally depressed. They wouldn't touch the suicides. The suicides usually hanged themselves with a belt.

One of Eddy's other jobs was the collection of prisoners from a railway siding eight miles away. They came from Russia and Denmark. Eddy needed four or five three-ton lorries to bring back those who couldn't walk. Many of the prisoners had lost their legs.

A Plymouth sergeant, Mad Jack, was over the top. All the Germans were terrified of him. Then there was Mad Bert. He was a huge man. One day he caught the two Germans who looked after the dining room stealing grapes. Boxes of grapes were cheap there – Eddy had sent some home to Vera. Mad Bert made the two Germans sit down and eat a whole box full. They were shitting pips for a week.

One day a big German from the KZ spat as Eddy walked by. He was big like a bladder of lard.

"You *stilstan*! You German bastard!" Eddy said.

"I understand English," the German sneered at him.

"You understand bang?" Eddy pressed his revolver against the fat man's forehead.

"*Ja, Ja, Ja*," the fat German said.

"Well I'll blow your fuckin' head off."

"For Chrissake Ed," Lionel said.

Lionel was a big Manchester man, used to make the rounds of the compound with Eddy. Lionel hated the Germans because they were the cause of his joining the Army and suffering its discipline. Any atrocities the Germans might have committed were by the way – they had made him join the Army.

"I'll give 'em discipline," Lionel said, and made them salute him. He would deliberately walk past them ten times and make them salute him every time.

At 4:00pm every day, Eddy, Old George and Lionel went to a little Austrian barber and his three assistants. They sat Lionel in a barber's chair that they'd made themselves, shaved him with an open razor, did his sideburns, eyebrows, and slapped on the scent. Then Old George would go, and lastly Eddy.

The first time he had watched the little Austrian stropping the open razor, and Eddy had thought how easy it would be for the Austrian to cut his throat. So Eddy drew his revolver and placed it ready on his lap.

"No gun," the Austrian said, shaking his head. "No gun, Bombardier, Sir."

"Well if you cut me bad," Eddy warned, "I may blow your head off. Understand?"

"No cut. No cut," the Austrian said.

Those were the only occasions Eddy drew his revolver while he was in the camp.

The new prisoners arrived at the railway station in cattle trucks. Most had come from Russia and were stinking. The cattle trucks stood about four feet off the ground. After being squashed so long into the trucks, the prisoners sometimes broke their legs if they jumped too quick.

Although Sergeant Major Stone was only supposed to be in charge of the *straaflager*, he came down to meet every train. He brought with him an Alsatian dog he'd got from the Police Guard, and a long heavy stick. As the flaps came down on the trucks he would beat their sides with a stick and yell: "*Schnell! Schnell! Schnell!*" the only German word he knew. With the dog barking, the German prisoners panicked and out they'd fall out, injuring themselves.

Sergeant Major Stone had spent all the war in the Military Police in charge of a glasshouse back in England.

Mad Jack from Plymouth was bomb-happy. He hated Sergeant Major Stone.

"That bastard!" he said every time Stone did it. "That bastard! That bastard shouldn't be down here. That bastard's no business being here."

Once out of the cattle trucks the Germans were lined up and marched back to the camp. Sergeant Major Stone would shout his only German word at those at the head of the column: "*Schnell! Schnell!*" And the faster those in front marched the faster they had to march along the rest of the column, until those in the rear had to run to keep up.

Eddy's job was to pick up only those Germans who couldn't march. One prisoner wouldn't go in the three-tonner, even though Eddy could see the blood coming out of his jackboots. The German wasn't yet going to give in, was going to walk it. Stone singled him out, and kept on at him.

The way to the camp lay through two small villages. As the column of prisoners passed through, the villagers would come out and jeer at the prisoners. Which didn't impress the British guards – they knew that during the occupation, many of the Belgians had been pally with the Germans. One woman in the first village came out every time with a coal hammer and tried to hit the prisoners.

Mad Jack this time said: "If that bloody woman comes out, I'll shoot her. It breaks all the bloody column. They could escape. Then we got that bastard Stone ..."

They came to the village. Mad Jack threatened the woman and she went back indoors. Mad Jack then turned on Sergeant Major Stone.

"You're a bloody disgrace to the British Army, you are. You've done no bloody fighting. You shouldn't even be down here with the Germans ..."

Sergeant Major Stone told Mad Jack where to get off. Mad Jack shot him – in the knee.

Mad Jack was court martialled, but he got away with it because he was nowhere near a hundred percent sane. All the other guards gave evidence on his behalf; and when the authorities discovered what Stone had been doing, the whole affair was hushed up.

Difka became friends with Eddy. He made Eddy's baby boy some toys. The prisoners would make anything. They did an oil painting – of a building on fire in Berlin. Not until Eddy examined it closely did he see that it was made up of lots of figures doing unspeakable things – even a little dog was portrayed masturbating. Difka made some wooden chickens that pecked at the ground when a string was pulled. Some other prisoners made Eddy two toy wooden horses and a cart.

They had men of eighty in the camp from the Volks – Home Guard – down to boys of twelve from the Kadets. Difka was an old German. He'd been in the German transport. His job in the camp was to count the prisoners, and he had a little hut just inside the gate. They counted them in batches of about a hundred. Difka was never wrong. Eddy gave him food and smokes on the quiet.

Eddy's interpreter was a Nazi paratrooper, a beer baron's son; and he thought that all ordinary German soldiers were pigs. The Bavarians were like that. Difka hated him. So did Eddy. The beer baron's son was only twenty-three, but he was clapped out physically, even though he looked alright. What annoyed Eddy most about him was that Eddy could never get a cigarette out before the beer baron's son was lighting it for him. The beer baron's son also told tales on the other prisoners. Difka didn't, was afraid to. There were many beatings in the camp at night.

One day Eddy gave some spuds to Difka. Difka cooked them.

"You want some, Bombardier?" he asked.

"I'll try a couple," Eddy said. The Germans fried their potatoes white and dripping with fat. The grease ran down their chins. Eddy couldn't eat them.

Another day Difka said to Eddy: "If I ask you to do something, will you keep it very quiet?"

"Yea. Why?"

"When you go to Brussels on your day off, would you go to this address and take my photo and this letter?"

"Why?"

"It is to a Jewish family. I helped some Jews to escape. If I'd been found out I wouldn't be here to tell you. Hitler didn't make any difference between foreigners and Germans. You were either for him or not."

Eddy went to see them. They lived in a smart part of Brussels, were suspicious at first; but they sent Difka a basket of food. Eddy gave it to him a bit at a time so that the other prisoners wouldn't notice.

In the camp they had a section of Luftwaffe pilots. They made model planes for the British troops. One told Eddy that he had been on raids over Plymouth and Exeter. Eddy told him that he was a bastard for doing that. The pilot replied that a British raid had killed his family, so it was all the same, madness really.

He explained how they had bombed Plymouth using a cartwheel route. They had gone around the rim of the cartwheel first, then in along the spokes. They had known that there was no ack-ack, and no opposition; and they had deliberately bombed the water plants first to hinder the fire-fighters. Plymouth had suffered more fire than bomb damage because they hadn't been able to put out the fires.

Eddy needed to build up some loot. His compound housed working prisoners who had passes to other compounds. Twenty Germans went out every morning to work in the offices. Fifty went down to clean the boots – everyone had their boots cleaned. Other prisoners went to the dining room, to do the cooking; and there were various other work details.

The sportsmaster, a prisoner, was in Eddy's compound. Before the war he had trained Ted Kid Lewis in England for the world middleweight boxing championship. He had a pass to go to any compound.

A carpenter, another prisoner, made a secret cupboard under the floor to Eddy's office. In there Eddy kept, at any one time, between twenty thousand and forty thousand cigarettes to trade for gold teeth. The cigarettes were smuggled into the prisoner compounds in the water cart. (Some other carpenters had made Eddy a watertight compartment inside the water cart. It only took them an hour.)

The sportsmaster would meet Eddy and report on how many gold teeth were available for trade and in which compounds. Eddy didn't ask where these teeth had come from. Some were the prisoners' own fillings. The others? They were of no use to the dead.

Both the sportsmaster and Eddy had a kit for testing the quality of the gold. Most of the teeth were eighteen carat. If they were good he paid three thousand cigarettes for each tooth, sometimes five thousand. It was the sportsmaster's job to deliver the cigarettes, from which he would take his cut.

Eddy took the gold teeth to a jeweller in Brussels, and used the money from that for his day-to-day living expenses, didn't draw any of his Army pay for himself. Although he had stacks of money, he couldn't send any home. So he started sending Vera silk underwear. Trouble was, he had no idea of size. A silk petticoat turned out to be no bigger than a vest. One pair of cami-knickers Vera couldn't get her legs into; another pair were like football shorts; and all the stockings were laddered. Only one pair of knickers fitted. The rest of his money Eddy spent on slap-up meals: he could buy black-market coupons.

Many of the prisoners had occupation marks on them. They were worth some money, could be sold on the Brussels black-market stock exchange. So Eddy got a few occupation marks together and set off for the stock exchange. Just before he arrived, the police raided it. Though that didn't stop another guard in another compound taking home ten thousand pounds. He carried it in his socks, in his boots, in his pack, even in his water bottle.

A Guards sergeant told Eddy about two of his soldiers who had been billeted in a house. The old woman who lived there kept on at them about something the Germans had buried in her garden. The two soldiers had been a bit chary about it, thinking it might have been mines or explosives. But she had kept on and on about it; and so, eventually, they took their shovels to the garden where they unearthed sixty thousand pounds of genuine English money, not counterfeit. That was the last seen of the two soldiers.

Everyone had a racket. Eddy knew another sergeant in Essel who got six years in military prison for his activities. He had been selling trainloads of coal belonging to the British Army, as well as truckloads of petrol.

One day the colonel in charge of the camp had all the British soldiers on parade. Colonel King was an ex-Guards officer, had originally been sent to discipline the British troops as well as the German prisoners. He had got the Germans to build the British soldiers a club. During the parade he told them that they would all have to start drawing pay.

"Only two men here have drawn pay in the last six months," he said. "Including the officers. Army Intelligence have now been sent here to find out what's been going on."

Afterwards Eddy told the Colonel that there were two men from Intelligence in his compound.

"How the hell did you know that? I didn't know that."

"They were drafted in as German prisoners," Eddy told him. "But they're in my compound."

"How do you know?"

"The Germans told me. They knew." Eddy had put them to cleaning the shithouse pits. They stayed three months, and left.

Some days Eddy and Lionel sat outside the compound while the prisoners constructed a road inside. The British Engineers hadn't been able to make a road that would stay up on the muddy earth. But there were some old masons amongst the German prisoners. They used tons of sand and little cobblestones, laid the cobblestones in an arc on the sand, then tapped them in. The sand had to be carried into the compound in tins and buckets – day after day. Some of the prisoners carrying out this work had no shoes, had their feet tied up in sacks.

Eddy sat watching them shuffling by, hating them for shuffling by and itching to shoot the bloody lot.

They had a Czech medical officer in the camp. If the British guards gave him a smart salute he treated them alright. In the camp hospital was a small convalescent ward for nerve cases – a big Nissen hut in which they could rest up for a couple of days. Eddy had to see the doctor regularly. The doctor would look into Eddy's eyes, examine his fingernails, and either tell him he was alright or to get into the ward for a few days rest. Eddy often went in when the weather was cold.

One German in Eddy's compound had more gold braid than a General. He never saluted anyone. Eddy asked Difka to find out who he was. It turned out that he was a German stationmaster and should never have been in there. Eddy got him transferred away.

Eddy had to help one Intelligence officer who arrived looking for war criminals. During questioning, this officer threatened the Nazis that he was going to knife them or beat them up; although he never actually touched them.

"They don't understand kindness, more's the pity, this kind of German," he told Eddy. He then ordered the Engineers to dig a tunnel behind the *straaflager*. The tunnel ended in a row of cubicles, with tiny holes drilled in the cubicle doors. The suspect Nazis were tied up and locked in the cubicles. Army Intelligence already had a good idea who the war criminals were.

"What's going to happen?" the tied-up Nazis asked Eddy.

"You know what you did to the Jews in Belsen? Well this is a gas chamber."

The Intelligence officer had made up a gas that smelled like Zyklon B but which wasn't poisonous. As soon as the Nazis heard that hissing into the cubicle they confessed. They had to know what it was to be afraid of it.

One day Eddy had to collect some German officers and take them to another camp in Ostend, about five miles from his own camp. Near that camp he met some Russians. They'd been stealing spuds – some of them were in trouble. Eddy chatted with them. They wouldn't say much, though, while their political sergeant was about. If they didn't come to heel on the party line they could be sent back to another regiment in Russia for re-education. Most of the Russians went mad for watches and clocks, would hold anyone up with a tommygun for their watch. If any Russian was caught looting, though, they were immediately shot.

Most of the Nazis in Eddy's compound were homosexuals. In the concentration camps they'd had no women. Their tailor was called the Jackdaw. He was beautiful.

The regiment sent Eddy those medals to which he was entitled – the 1939 Star, the France & Germany Star, and the General Service Star. He had to wear them when he went out. It was an offence not to.

They asked Eddy to sign on for another five years, promised him the rank of RSM – a crown above his stripes – if he did. He turned it down.

The camp had its own orchestra. They played in a different compound every day. Wednesday was Eddy's concert day. At 2:00pm all the prisoners would file into the building. Sometimes

Lionel went with Eddy, sometimes George. Although George more often stayed in the office, preferred to be on the gate.

The new *lagerfuhrer* was a barrister, had not been a Nazi. To the men he was stern but fair. He was a clever man, and told Eddy all about the war in Russia.

The *lagerfuhrer* would already be in the concert hall with his assistants when Eddy and Lionel entered. And as soon as Eddy and Lionel came, in the orchestra would strike up 'Roll Out The Barrel ...' and Eddy and Lionel would walk grandly down the aisle. Eddy would then turn to face the audience, lift his hand and say: "Begin."

Nothing started until Eddy lifted his hand and gave the word. It was like being King. Eddy loved it.

There was always a scramble for the seats behind Eddy and Lionel so that the prisoners could pick up the kippings – the dog ends from their cigarettes. Those seats were sold on the black-market.

Eddy could soon tell which of the concert comedians came from Berlin – they had a sort of Cockney lilt to their accents. And the jokes came thick and fast – most, Eddy guessed, about the British.

"I wish I knew what those bastards were saying about us," Eddy said to the *lagerfuhrer*.

"No, it's quite alright. I wouldn't allow that."

"What we call taking the mickey," Eddy said.

"Oh no, I wouldn't allow any of the taking of the mickey," the *lagerfuhrer* reassured.

Eddy still had his doubts.

One day Eddy had to go to the General Hospital in Brussels – the one where he'd first been taken after his collapse – for his final medical. The doctor was in a room opposite the lavatories. Outside the door was the doctor's medical orderly. The medical orderly was given the doctor's report as the patient left.

Everybody had a racket. The medical orderly's was information – selling the doctor's reports at five hundred francs each. On the report would be stated how much pension the patient was recommended and why. After seeing the doctor, Eddy went into the lavatory. The orderly handed over the report and Eddy paid the five hundred francs.

On the report Eddy was recommended for a fifty percent pension. The man in the next lavatory had had a testicle shot off. But because he still had one testicle left, he was only recommended a twenty-five percent pension.

While Eddy was waiting, Unity Mitford, a smart piece, had been brought in to see the doctor. She was being held in a prison nearby.

Eddy's demobilisation came early – almost a year after the end of the war. Because he was a builder he came out on the B-release scheme. He caught the train to Ostend, stayed there two days, then caught the ferry. This time, when he landed in England they were all searched by customs.

Eighteen

Eddy often disappeared. Vera knew where to find him – at her mother and father's. Eddy liked to get Ned talking about the wealthy Strubins family, listen to tales about the toffs – a far remove from the war.

"I'll take the babe out in the pram," Eddy would say. Reluctantly, Vera would make up the pram. Then wait.

Eddy and the baby would be gone for hours. Vera would wonder if Eddy had jumped over a cliff, or forgotten where he'd left the pram ... And she didn't like to make excuses to stop him taking the baby, nor drop everything to go with him, in case she made it obvious that she didn't trust him.

The baby got nappy rash from teething. Vera paid to see the doctor who prescribed some ointment. But the ointment was too strong. The baby got infantile eczema. Every night the baby had to wear special gloves and have his hands strapped to his sides. The baby did not cry. He shouted. Eddy had nightmares.

Eddy had a month's holiday, after which he was sent to work for a Mr Fair, who lived out in Chelston. Most of the work was on big houses, repairing roofs.

As the others of the old crowd were demobbed and came home, each had a party. Eddy, who had been the life and soul of every party before the war, went to none of them. All he wanted was to work. To work it out of him.

The Canadian doctor had told him: "The only one who'll get you over it is you."

In the evenings he sat in an armchair and stared into space while Vera moved around him. He didn't speak.

Then he went fishing, got back into the band. Though he still wouldn't go to the doctor, Vera went. The doctor told her that he couldn't do anything unless Eddy came himself. And Eddy had been recommended for a pension – which he refused to collect.

Although Eddy was fine with Vera's mother and father, he fell out with pretty near everyone else. He was very touchy. The only other man whose company he could abide was a Welsh bricklayer who had the same nerve complaint.

Eddy would meet him in the Palk Arms after work. The Welshman's family wanted him to go to Bristol and have part of his brain removed.

"Why don't you come back bricklaying?" Eddy asked him. "Work your way out of it." He was a good bricklayer.

"Oh, I can't. They want me to go up there and have my brain touched. And they don't know how it'll turn out."

Two weeks later the Welshman was having a drink with his brothers in the Palk Arms and he went to the lavatories. His brothers decided he was taking too long. They found him with his throat cut from ear to ear.

Vera took the baby to Solomons for a check-up. Solomons was the school doctor. He looked hard at Vera. "Why haven't you had anything done about this boy?"

"How can I?"

" 'Course you can. Could have had this done ages ago. A proper mess." Vera sat down and cried, explained to him what had happened.

"I'll get this seen to right away." The next week the baby was in Exeter.

In Exeter there were dozens of other malformed children – some without mouths, some with no noses. The doctor they saw was called FitzGibbons. The baby by now had two hard lumps in his top lip.

"My God. Who did this?"

Vera told him the name of the doctor.

"But he's been retired for years. He's sewn the muscle, pulled his nose out of shape." He was furious. "It'll have to be ripped out."

He explained to Vera and Eddy that it would have been easier had it been a proper hare lip, or even a cleft palate – he could have built that up from scratch. But with only a split, and one that had been botched ... he would do his best.

And Vera and Eddy discovered that there were hundreds of babies who had been born malformed during the war. For no obvious reason. Vera and Eddy, like most of the other parents, had no history of malformity in their families. Nor was it just one class – one of the doctors there had a son who had been born malformed. Just another aspect of the war, he said.

Eddy had been put on the Army's Z Reserve, was entitled to two pensions – one for the finger he'd lost in Harrogate, and one for his back injury. But first he had to undergo another medical to claim them; and he was sick of doctors and medicals. He had seen too many doctors, wanted nothing more to do with them. Vera kept on at him to claim his pension. He wouldn't – not if it meant that he had to go for yet another medical.

Big Whitey, the shipwright, was in the same mental state as Eddy. Saturday mornings, Eddy met him down at Stockman's, a café by the harbour. All the fishing boys met there. Whitey was a bachelor.

"I'm going to have this bloody medical," he told Eddy one Saturday.

"I'll see you down here next Saturday then," Eddy said.

Next Saturday morning Big Whitey came into Stockman's laughing all over his face.

"How'd you get on?" Eddy asked him.

"Rough," Whitey said. "I goes in up there. And there's all these four sat at a bloody great table. And me out this side. One bastard's asking me this. Another bastard's asking me that. And like you said, you don't know what the bloody hell they been writing about you. Do 'e? So I picked the table up and said: 'Stick your bloody pension!' "

THE END

For The Duration (Where known) ...

Frank Andrews – worked in a factory in Buckinghamshire

Sam Avery – killed in Coventry working on bomb disposal

Dick Berry – became a major

George Browning – continued in Home Guard

Cyril Blackler – invalided out of Engineers with bad back

Harold Bradcock – worked on bomb damage

Percy Bragg – continued in Home Guard

Charles Bran – knighted for his war effort

Harry Bunch – worked on bomb damage in London

Bill Clemens – continued farming, reserved occupation

Captain Dampier – continued in Home Guard

George Downer – served in paratroops

Cyril Drew – in the ARP

Les Ellis – served in the desert

Eli Mannen – killed in Burma

Frank Endicott – served in Engineers

Bert Ewens – served in Army band

Jack Fagin – continued in Home Guard

Reg Hayman – continued in Home Guard, possibly joined RAF

Baron Hingston – made sergeant in charge of pigeons

Mac – served in RAF in Gibraltar

Jack Martin – served in Engineers

Major Moore – continued in Home Guard

Muriel & Roy – Roy served in RAF

Cyril Perry – went from ack-ack to Redcaps, made provost sergeant

Norman Poke – served in RAF

Ron Pouilly – served in RAF, awarded Distinguished Conduct Medal

Bert Rook – served in the Army

Herb Sarahs – served in RN on Mermansk convoys

Jack Shapley – continued in Home Guard

Len Toms – served as bricklayer in RN

Jim Tozer – continued in Home Guard

Mr Truman – continued in Home Guard

Postscript

After the war, Vera and Eddy had two more children, Stephanie and Stephen, in quick succession. To support them Eddy worked as a bricklayer during the day, went out with the band in the evenings; and at weekends, as the doctor ordered, he went fishing – taking the whole family with him. Vera and Eddy also took up old time dancing, won medals. And occasionally he and Vera went to parties with the old crowd.

To make ends meet, as soon as the babies were old enough, Vera took up hairdressing at home again. So that Eddy's father could come to live with them, the family moved out of Congella Road and into a bigger house in Reddenhill Road.

When Eddy's father remarried and moved out, Vera started taking in bed & breakfast holiday-makers in the summer and she returned to hairdressing in the Co-op.

Living in London in the Sixties, I became friends with Chris. He was at Central Art College. I had just left the Merchant Navy (having had first-hand experience of war's confusion in the Indo-Pakistan conflict of '64/'65). In London I was a scaffolder, then a computer operator, and was about to decide to become a writer. In the meantime I spent drinking weekends with Chris in Torquay, met Vera and Eddy, Steve and Stephanie.

In 1976, Stephanie and I set up home together in Somerset. Vera and Eddy, semi-retired now, came to stay with us for weeks at a time. Which was when I came by the idea of taping their war stories.

Eddy readily agreed.

Vera, happy to tell a funny story, even happier to be told one, kept her own counsel on more serious matters. She preferred to spend her evenings playing cards or scrabble, and always for money.

Eventually she let herself be persuaded. But that was only the beginning. Keeping them both to the subject took more tact than I previously considered myself capable of, while pinning them down to exact dates turned out to be near impossible.

These days I expect that Eddy would have been diagnosed as suffering from post traumatic stress disorder and offered the appropriate talking therapies. Such therapies not then being on offer, Eddy simply talked; and his talking, his continual relating of events, both momentous and trivial, were – I believe – his way of making some meaningful order of all that had befallen him in his life.

Over the subsequent years I transcribed the tapes, returning to Vera and Eddy, while both were still alive, for more details, and for – hope beyond hope – clarification.

When I had first started to collect material from them my intention had been for the book to become a documentary – to retell the stories in the first person as both had told them to me, for it to be their record of a little bit of history.

The Second World War was a war that had involved everyone, not just a few generals and politicians, but every member of every family. It had been a war fought, in Europe, literally on our doorsteps. I had become tired of the myth and legend being built around it, had wanted to show what that war had actually done to one family.

The fear of libel, however, is so strong in this country that Vera asked me to present the story as fiction. That, though, would have defeated my purpose, for many of the events described herein could then have been dismissed as the work of a novelist's

240

imagination, and so have lost their impact. Consequently, for a while, I had to promise to disguise identities and to omit certain names before Vera and Eddy would tell me any more of their war experiences.

Nor had I realised, when embarking upon this project, so naïve a writer was I, just how limited were the publishing opportunities for war memoirs of this kind. The few publishers who did declare an interest in such material I quickly found to be vanity publishers, cashing in on the stories, like Eddy's, demanding to be told; each author, like Eddy, having to tell, trying to get across to anyone who would listen, who would read, the importance of what had happened to them; and defeated every time by the enormity of it, by the incomprehension of their unreceptive audience ... When one of these unprincipled publishers carelessly disappeared along with the manuscript, I reprinted the original, made photocopies for the family, and considered the enterprise closed.

No story, though, can ever said to be finished.

After a long illness, at the very end still more concerned for others than for herself, Vera died in 1989. Eddy limped along for several more years, emphysema and his faulty heart combined almost doing for him several times. On each readmission to Torbay hospital the staff was amazed to see him still alive.

On one of those admissions another patient recognised Eddy's name. He told Eddy that he had some papers of his. He had been a relation of Eddy's father's second wife. In among the papers, when they arrived, was Eddy's mother and father's wedding certificate, which was dated some time after Eddy's birth.

"Bit much," Eddy said, "to have to wait till you're eighty-four to find out you're a bastard."

In one of those later hospitalisations, fighting for every heartbeat, every breath, Eddy told Stephanie of a French girl writing to Vera after the war and telling Vera of her love for Eddy.

For once, apart from saying Vera had been none too pleased about it, Eddy wouldn't say much more.

But .... no story can ever be complete unto itself, that neatly finished. One day, these years later, I approached another publisher on another matter, just happened to mention that I'd also written a book about the Second World War.

They asked to see the manuscript of Vera & Eddy's War ...

Sam Smith

Glossary

Ack-Ack – a Bofors gun, anti-aircraft; or the sky-burst results of anti-aircraft fire

balls-up – fiasco

bloke – a man

bollocking – a telling off

bollocks – testicles

bugger – (Devon colloq.) beggar

bully beef – corned beef

chary – wary

crabs – pubic lice

'crack her jaw' – talk posh, upper-class way of speaking

daft – stupid

doolally-tap – gone slightly mad

fag(s) – cigarette(s)

fizzer – a charge

flap-happy – battle hysteria, see doolally-tap

French letter – condom

goolies – testicles

Hore-Belisha, Leslie – Minister of Transport 1931-7, inventor of the 'Belisha Beacon' road-crossing warning light and in charge of logistics during the wartime coalition government

jacksy – backside, arse, ass

kippings – dog-ends, butts, fag-ends

knackers – testicles

knackered – tired

lance-jack – lance corporal

Mary-Anne – fusspot (poss. effeminate)

Mustard – hot stuff

pongo – any army personnel

pullover – a jersey, woollen top

queer cove – oddball

randy – sexually aroused, or person who is constantly in such condition

rookie – learner, new recruit

scrumpy – Devon rough cider

shagging – sexual congress

skiving – shirking

spiv – a flashy black marketeer

spondoolicks – wages, money

Spring-heeled Jack – gym instructor

spud – potato

swaling – burning dry vegetation, mostly heather or corn stubble

tiffy – artificer

tip-and-run – the arbitrary dropping of bombs before a quick retreat

Torquay United – a football (soccer) team

wop – sexual congress

yek – a defecation

Also Available from BeWrite Books

Crime
Sweet Molly Maguire – Terry Houston

The surreal world of a mean city newspaper swallowed the very toughest or spat them out. This circus of hopeless drunks and heartless back-stabbers was no place for Sweet Molly Maguire. She died, raped and pregnant, and didn't merit a single line of print. But for one reporter, her death wasn't the end of just another story. It was the opening sentence in a search for something rare in the news room ... the bitter truth.

Paperback   ISBN 1-904224-05-9
          $13.50 US/ £9.80 UK/ $21.24 Canada/ €15.55 Europe
Ebook   ISBN 1-904224-01-6
          $6.55 US/ £4.80 UK/ $10.40 Canada/ €7.65 Europe
CD – Rom   ISBN 1-904224-06-7
          $10.25 US/ £7.50 UK/ $16.25 Canada/ €11.90 Europe

Horror
Chill – Terri Pine, Peter Lee, Andrew Müller

Dim the lights. Tug up the quilt so that only your eyes are visible. Now, slip into the dark, dark night of this world's greatest masters of macabre. Try not to sleep. Watch for moving shadows. And – whatever happens – *don't* get out of bed ... you may catch your very death ...

Paperback   ISBN 1-904224-08-3
          $13.50 US/ £9.80 UK/ $21.24 Canada/ €15.55 Europe
Ebook   ISBN 1-904224-03-2
          $6.55 US/ £4.80 UK/ $10.40 Canada/ €7.65 Europe
CD – Rom   ISBN 1-904224-11-3
          $10.25 US/ £7.50 UK/ $16.25 Canada/ €11.90 Europe

Crime
Marks – Sam Smith

George Hawkins is a small town detective – low on ambition, lower on glamour. The most exciting part of life is making midnight chalk marks on tyres and roads ... when the marks still match up the following morning, he has proof that someone's been playing away from home. But George's humdrum life is turned upside down within a single day when he witnesses a hit-and-run, his house is burgled, and his girlfriend disappears, leaving him prime suspect.

Paperback   ISBN 1-904224-09-1
          $13.50 US/ £9.80 UK/ $21.24 Canada/ €15.55 Europe
Ebook   ISBN 1-904224-02-4
          $6.55 US/ £4.80 UK/ $10.40 Canada/ €7.65 Europe
CD – Rom   ISBN 1-904224-17-2
          $10.25 US/ £7.50 UK/ $16.25 Canada/ €11.90 Europe

Autobiography
The Golden Locket – A Post-Edwardian Childhood – Dorothy Kathleen Kirby

It may not have mattered to Dorothy Kathleen Kirby that she didn't live to see the book she had written. She had *lived* the memories between its covers. In nine decades that saw the Flanders trenches and the terror attack on Manhattan, Dorothy focused on the simple detail of everyday life, and discovered a wonderful world. Page by delightful page, you cannot help but be struck by the truth that counting blessings one by one can produce a mighty sum.

Paperback   ISBN 1-904224-07-5
          $13.50 US/ £9.80 UK/ $21.24 Canada/ €15.55 Europe
Ebook   ISBN 1-904224-00-8
          $6.55 US/ £4.80 UK/ $10.40 Canada/ €7.65 Europe
CD – Rom   ISBN 1-904224-10-5
          $10.25 US/ £7.50 UK/ $16.25 Canada/ €11.90 Europe

Crime
The Knotted Cord – Alistair Kinnon

The body of a naked young boy hanging in a dusty barn stirs sickening feelings of déjà vu in the detective. As he untangles each knot in the tangled cord of his investigation, he uncovers a murderous thread ... and police prejudices which may have allowed previous killings to happen ... not to mention his own guilt! **Alistair Kinnon** has written much more than a tense, psychological crime novel -- his twisting plot takes the reader into the murky world of child sex-for-sale ... the parent's darkest nightmare and the child's greatest threat.

Paperback   ISBN 1-904224-12-1
          $13.50 US/ £9.80 UK/ $21.24 Canada/ €15.55 Europe
Ebook   ISBN 1-904224-04-1
          $6.55 US/ £4.80 UK/ $10.40 Canada/ €7.65 Europe
CD – Rom   ISBN 1-904224-13-X
          $10.25 US/ £7.50 UK/ $16.25 Canada/ €11.90 Europe

Fantasy Humour
Zolin – A Rockin' Good Wizard – Barry Ireland

Worlds go along happily side-by-side in their own dimensiverses ... until they accidentally bump into each other. Then a wild Glasgow rock band, randy witches, dragons for hire and kings and queens end up rocking where they should have been rolling. And bewildered apprentice wizard, Zolin, is piggy in the middle. **Barry Ireland's** book is to Fantasy what The Hitchhiker's Guide to the Galaxy was to Sci Fi. An adult fairy tale!

Paperback   ISBN 1-904224-19-9
          $13.50 US/ £9.80 UK/ $21.24 Canada/ €15.55 Europe
Ebook   ISBN 1-904224-18-0
          $6.55 US/ £4.80 UK/ $10.40 Canada/ €7.65 Europe
CD – Rom   ISBN 1-904224-20-2
          $10.25 US/ £7.50 UK/ $16.25 Canada/ €11.90 Europe

Romance
A Different Kind of Love – Jay Mandal

More than any other collection, this thought-provoking work will introduce the heterosexual reader to the meaning of *true* gay love, and will afford the gay reader a sigh of relief that – at last – a popular, respected and serious author has cast aside threadbare issues of hatred, brutality, perversion, prejudice and misunderstanding to get to the very heart of the matter ... the honest to goodness love between human beings who ask little more of life than that.

Paperback   ISBN 1-904224-40-7
          $13.50 US/ £9.80 UK/ $21.24 Canada/ €15.55 Europe
Ebook   ISBN 1-904224-39-9
          $6.55 US/ £4.80 UK/ $10.40 Canada/ €7.65 Europe
CD – Rom   ISBN 1-904224-41-5
          $10.25 US/ £7.50 UK/ $16.25 Canada/ €11.90 Europe

General
Odie Dodie – The Life and Crimes of a Travelin' Preacher Man – Lad Moore

Lad Moore builds a collection of tales of stark reality, hanging on the wobbly hook of a phony, money grubbing, licentious gospel-peddler, Odie Dodie and his unholy glory bus.
    Never since Steinbeck and Hemingway has an author written so tightly, entertainingly and honestly about what matters most ... The simple truth!

Paperback   ISBN 1-904224-08-3
          $13.50 US/ £9.80 UK/ $21.24 Canada/ €15.55 Europe
Ebook   ISBN 1-904224-03-2
          $6.55 US/ £4.80 UK/ $10.40 Canada/ €7.65 Europe
CD – Rom   ISBN 1-904224-11-3
          $10.25 US/ £7.50 UK/ $16.25 Canada/ €11.90 Europe

Thriller
Blood Money – Azam Gill
A starkly realistic novel of love and hate in the murky world of international terrorism, mercenary soldiering, dirty banking and underground government agencies. Gill, with the skill of a master story teller and the authority of an actual former insider, writes a gritty story of star-crossed love against a scenario strikingly close to that which may have led up to the attack on the Twin Towers ... and a war far from over.

Paperback   ISBN 1-904224-91-1
            $13.50 US/ £9.80 UK/ $21.24 Canada/ €15.55 Europe
Ebook   ISBN 1-904224-90-3
            $6.55 US/ £4.80 UK/ $10.40 Canada/ €7.65 Europe
CD – Rom   ISBN 1-904224-92-X
            $10.25 US/ £7.50 UK/ $16.25 Canada/ €11.90 Europe

Crime
Porlock Counterpoint – Sam Smith
Sam Smith goes one step beyond the psychological crime novel when he places cynical cops to, like the reader, observe the counterpoint between two levels of criminal. The middle-aged, middle-class couple smuggling hard drugs for their avaricious dreams and the desperate young couple who 'borrow' their car simply to get to hospital in time for the birth of their baby. The quartet may never meet ... but their lives, worlds apart in terms of social rank and the definition of 'crime', collide with shattering results.

Paperback   ISBN 1-904224-15-6
            $13.50 US/ £9.80 UK/ $21.24 Canada/ €15.55 Europe
Ebook   ISBN 1-904224-14-8
            $6.55 US/ £4.80 UK/ $10.40 Canada/ €7.65 Europe
CD – Rom   ISBN 1-904224-16-4
            $10.25 US/ £7.50 UK/ $16.25 Canada/ €11.90 Europe

Short Stories
The Miller Moth – Mike Broemmel
The miller moth flutters through Mike Broemmel's pages like a phantom - sometimes benevolent, sometimes threatening. A shade of human life itself. Characters you'll meet are ordinary people in ordinary situations - made extraordinary with the touch of a modern Steinbeck. You will recognize yourself, family and neighbours in this collection of deceptively simple stories crafted with the intricacy, delicacy and humanity of a master wordsmith.

Paperback   ISBN 1-904224-15-6
            $13.50 US/ £9.80 UK/ $21.24 Canada/ €15.55 Europe
Ebook   ISBN 1-904224-14-8
              $6.55 US/ £4.80 UK/ $10.40 Canada/ €7.65 Europe
CD – Rom   ISBN 1-904224-16-4
            $10.25 US/ £7.50 UK/ $16.25 Canada/ €11.90 Europe

N.B The price for paperback and CD-Rom excludes postage and packaging.
Prices correct at time of press.

All the above titles are available from

www.bewrite.net

Printed in the United Kingdom
by Lightning Source UK Ltd.
1535